DON'T FEAR THE REAPER

Garry Kay

Also by Garry Kay

Break Free
The Door
Jagger Black

For Ginny, Hannah and Sam

1 ... **Stop the clock**

Day of the crash, Wednesday, April 11, 1984:
The Grim Reaper opened the front panel of
his tall white grandfather clock and stopped
the pendulum. The fingers on the dial
stopped. The screaming stopped. The sound
of ripping metal and crunching rock stopped.
The sound of crying children stopped, but an
echo lingered as he turned from the clock and
sat at his burgundy velvet chaise longue.

The bus was surprisingly intact after
rolling twice on the tight bend which followed
the cliff above the Corfiot resort of
Palaiokastritsa. It had come to rest upside
down on its roof half over the edge of the
cliff. It was 300 feet above the jagged rocks
that lined the bay.

The Grim Reaper looked down at Mary
Teal, who lay unconscious in her husband's
arms. Before the clock stopped, Gordon Teal
had been pressing the palm of his hand
against a gash on Mary's leg to try and stop
the bleeding.

Grim crossed his legs and leant back. He
rested one hand on the arm of the chair, took a
deep breath and waved at Mary with his other
hand.

'Sit with me a minute,' he said, with warmth. He was a young man, 20 years old with untidy fair hair. He wore black corduroy trousers and a sports jacket.

'You're Jack String from The Southside Gazette aren't you?' said Mary as she stood up and edged slowly towards the chaise longue.

'Please. Have a seat.' He patted the burgundy fabric at his side and nodded gently. 'I am the Grim Reaper.' His voice was soft and re-assuring.

Mary sat down and said nothing. She looked around the roof of the upturned bus. She could see fear in the eyes of survivors, who had realised that the bus could fall off the cliff at any moment and kill them all. She saw vacant looks in the eyes of those who had been killed in the initial impact of the crash. She looked at Jack String.

'Am I dead?'

The Grim Reaper turned away from Mary, raised his eyebrows and looked towards her flaccid body lying in her husband's arms.

'Not yet.'

She drew breath. Her mind was racing. Only moments ago, she had been focussed on the ticking of the grandfather clock. She heard the screams of her fellow passengers, but the loudest noise was the clock. Until it stopped. Then it all went quiet. Even the pain stopped. And there was Jack String, the newspaper reporter she had met in her back garden a month ago in England.

She lived in a cottage on the sharp bend of a main road. It was a deceptively sharp bend and there were frequent accidents. The day she met Jack was the day she cradled a dying man in her arms. His car had landed in her duck pond and she had been first on the scene and waited 20 minutes for the paramedics to ease the man out of her blood-soaked arms. He later died on his way to the hospital.

'What did the man say to you before he died?'

Mary looked away. She was reliving the horror. It had been the seventh crash on the bend by her house, the fourth vehicle to slide into her garden and the second fatality.

'He kept saying, "Why me?" over and over.'

'Anything else?'

Mary couldn't think.

Grim helped her. 'He told you he had too much to do. He told you people relied on him and he was too young to die.'

Mary frowned and looked at the young man beside her. 'You were there weren't you?'

Grim nodded slowly. 'I was in the back of the car talking to the dying man. We both watched you cradle his body in the front of the car.'

Mary's eyes widened.

Grim continued. 'You couldn't have saved him. He was on my list three days before the crash. I had very little choice.'

Mary was quiet again, her mind still racing. She had a bad feeling. Then she turned back to the Grim Reaper.

'But you did have a choice?'

'I had three people on my list that day. But I only had a quota of one to fill.'

Mary waited for him to continue.

'You and Gordon were also on my list. You had both been in the garden around the time of the crash. I could have chosen either one of you, but I chose the driver.'

Mary stared long into Jack's eyes. She needed answers.

'Why the driver?'

'I didn't like him.'

Mary looked shocked. 'Is that it? Nothing deep and meaningful?'

Jack shook his head. 'No. Nothing. I just didn't like him. I watched him for a few days and he annoyed me. He was selfish.'

'Have you been watching me?'

'Oh yes. And not just you. I've been with all 49 people on this bus for the whole week of your holiday. I was even on the flight over from Heathrow. It's all part of my job. Don't always have the time for research and I'm not obliged to research anyway. I just get a quota and it's up to me who I fill it with from any given situation and any given list.'

'So you were allocated this bus crash.'

'Yup.' Jack nodded.

'So we're all on your list?'

'All 49.'

'And we all die?'

'Nope. Just 16. Well, maybe just 16. Could be more. But not less.'

'Which 16?'

Now the Grim Reaper looked thoughtful. 'Well. That's the difficult thing. I dunno yet. Haven't decided.'

'So why are you talking to me?'

Jack grimaced.

Mary looked at herself in her husband's arms, but when she looked back at the Grim Reaper, he was no longer Jack String. He no longer looked reassuring. Her mouth was dry. 'You're the man who died in my garden.'

'I'm the Grim Reaper.'

Mary started to feel pain. 'Am I going to die?'

'You have a ruptured spleen, a broken leg and you're bleeding heavily.'

'Sounds like a "yes".'

'Not necessarily.'

'What about Gordon?'

'Mostly bumps and bruises, but he has a small blood clot working its way towards his lungs. He's in pain. And it will get much worse if the clot reaches his lungs.'

'So were both going to die?'

'Hmmm. Again … not necessarily.'

'What then?'

'I've got to take one of you.'

'Why?' pleaded Mary with thinly disguised anger.

The Grim Reaper rubbed his chin in thought and leant back in what was now a lilac armchair. 'A number of reasons.' He raised his blood soaked arm. He still had all the injuries from the crash in Mary's garden. 'Firstly, you have both been on my list three times each and I have already spared you both more than I should have done, and secondly, there are some good people on this bus who I think deserve to live more than you. Harsh I know, but that's the way it is.'

Mary took in what he said before asking, 'Which one of us then?'

Grim shrugged his shoulders. 'Can't decide. It's too close to call.'

'What you gonna do then? Toss a coin?'

'No.' He paused looking deep into Mary's eyes. 'I'm going to let you and Gordon choose between you.'

She took a sharp breath and turned to Gordon, who was stood facing her just to the right of their two bodies.

'We're not discussing it Mary. I'm older than you. I'm going.' Gordon was adamant.

'Just a minute.' Mary turned to the Grim Reaper for help, but he was gone. The lilac chair was gone. Just the clock remained. The pendulum didn't move but it looked impatient. She turned back to Gordon. It was three days until his 65th birthday. He had promised her a bottle of champagne purchased with his state pension. He had been looking forward to his retirement for years.

'I've got a ruptured spleen and broken leg. I should go.'

'I've got a blood clot heading for my lungs.' Gordon stepped over a dead woman and reached his open arms towards Mary.

They held each other tight and closed their eyes.

After a while Gordon whispered softly. 'I couldn't bear to live without you. So I'm being selfish. Let me go.'

Mary wasn't having it. She pushed him away and shouted 'no' before a smile spread across her face.

Gordon's face also lit up. They were no longer on the bus. They were in an empty two-up-two-down terraced house in Southside, a town of around 40,000 people just south of London. Their footsteps echoed as they walked across the bare floorboards.

'18 Granville Terrace,' said Gordon with pride. 'Our first house together.'

'Blimey.' Mary couldn't stop smiling. 'I loved this house. Must have been over 30 years ago.'

'34 years.' Gordon had a good memory for dates.

'Mortgaged up to our eyeballs,' Mary remembered surprisingly fondly as it had been quite a struggle at the time.

'Worth it though Babe. I hated that rented flat.'

Mary walked through to the kitchen. 'Gordon.' She called. 'Look. Do you remember this work surface?'

'Yes Mary. I do believe Nigel was conceived on that work surface.'

As he reached for her hand, there was a knock at the door. Gordon walked through and fumbled with the latch before struggling to pull the door open, until he remembered it had to be lifted slightly while pulling.

'Mr Teal. Found it eventually,' beamed a tall round-faced man of about 40 in brown overalls.

'Fat Harry. How are you?' Gordon faced back along the entrance hall. 'Mary. It's Fat Harry.'

Fat Harry looked a little surprised by his warm greeting. '2pm as promised. Right. Let's get busy.'

He started carrying in Gordon and Mary's furniture from the flat.

'Through here Harry,' shouted Mary as she spotted their floral sofa.

Gordon and Mary sat on their sofa in their first house arm in arm and wallowed in nostalgia as Fat Harry and his son carried all their meagre possessions into their new home.

'I wish you'd chuck that dentist's chair.' Mary had never liked it.

'I will. I promise. When we can afford better.'

'How many times have I heard that?'

'Okay Mary? How about that blue Formica chest of drawers. It's disgusting. When are you going to get rid of that?'

'When we can afford better.'

'We're never going to agree.'

'We never agree on anything.' Mary smiled and kissed Gordon on the cheek. 'Why did we get married?'

'I don't know the answer to that question,' Gordon replied playfully.

Fat Harry placed a cheese plant in the corner next to the sofa. 'That's your lot. I'd best leave you to it.'

They both thanked him and Gordon shook his hand before closing the front door behind him.

Gordon sat in his dentist's chair and pumped the lever until he was almost lying flat.

Mary opened the doors on her Formica chest of drawers before sitting back on the sofa.

They both looked up surprised as there was another knock at the door, but before either of them stood up, Fat Harry let himself in. 'Nearly forgot this,' he shouted before struggling through the door with a tall white grandfather clock.

'That's not ours.' Mary didn't recognise it.

Fat Harry stood it in an alcove by the fireplace. 'Oh dear. It's stopped.' He pulled open the front panel and gave the pendulum a little nudge.

Gordon pressed firmly on Mary's leg to try and stop the bleeding. He couldn't tell if she was breathing or not. The screaming was deafening and the sound of ripping metal sent a shiver down his spine as he looked back through the smashed rear window, which alternated slowly from a view of clear blue sky to a mixture of sky and the tops of the hills on the far side of the bay.

2 ... **Spiros Gekas**

Day of the crash, Wednesday, April 11, 1984: Spiros Gekas strutted along the main drag in Sidari, the most lively resort in the north west of Corfu. He stuck his chest out and bounced along with the confidence of a man who loved women and could usually take his pick. He was 35 years old, wore shiny polished black shoes, tight blue jeans and a black dress shirt open at the collar. He had black hair, gelled and brushed back, a heavy gold chain around

his neck and mirrored sunglasses o
deep brown eyes.

He spoke good English with a
Greek accent, which was always p
the holiday-makers who flocked to
looking for a good time in the countless bars
and clubs that lined the main street. He was a
coach driver and had half an hour to kill
before taking a crowd of tourists to the
airport.

There were very few tourists on the
island. The chartered flights run by package
holiday firms hadn't started, but a few
determined holidaymakers had made their
way to the island via Athens using Greek
scheduled flights. In a bid to boost trade, the
airline had hired Spiros to run a transfer
service from the north west resorts down to
the airport.

It was early afternoon and Spiros headed
for his favourite bar, Joe's British Pub. The
sun was shining through patchy grey clouds,
but it had been a bad day for Spiros. His
tangled web of women had started to come
undone and driving a bus full of tourists was
the last thing he wanted to do.

Although the main drag was packed with
bars, clubs, fast food outlets, supermarkets
and souvenir shops, most were still closed up

winter or receiving a fresh lick of paint for the new season. Joe's was one of only two bars that stayed open all year. There were plenty of tavernas in Corfiot villages where the locals lived, but the resort of Sidari was a lonely place in April.

Spiros jumped up the three steps at the entrance between two mature palm trees and weaved his way through the glass-topped wicker tables to Sonia, Joe's wife, who was checking through the accounts at a table near the outside veranda bar.

There were no customers or staff.

'Sonia, Sonia, the most beautiful girl in Sidari,' Spiros whispered softly as he hugged her from behind her seat and gently kissed her neck.

'You're such a tart Spiros,' she laughed.

'I was, but I'm a new man now. I've come to take you away from all this.' He ran his fingers through her blonde hair.

Joe and Sonia had opened their bar in Sidari after running a pub in Essex. They had dreamed of a leisurely life in the sun, but five years of extremely hard work and extremely low profit had left them dreaming of a quiet life back in Essex.

She faced him and held his hand. 'You'd do it wouldn't you?'

'Right now babe.' He took off his sunglasses and looked her in the eye. 'Let's go.'

'Spiros darling.' She gently bit her lip. 'Before we even got off the island, you would have jumped into bed with somebody else.'

'Not with you on my arm,' he reassured her.

'And what about my husband?'

'Sorry. No room in the car,' he joked. 'And, besides, I'm better looking than he is.'

'And what about your mistress?'

'I'll leave her for you.'

'And your wife and three kids?'

'They'll manage on their own.'

She patted him on the shoulder. 'I think I'll stick with Joe, but don't stop asking. It always brightens my day.'

'Okay babe. How about a beer then?'

Sonia headed for the bar just as Joe came through from the back.

'Ya-sou,' shouted Spiros. He jumped up and hugged Joe. 'Have a beer with me friend. I'm drowning my sorrows. Your wife won't run away with me and I've asked her every day for the past five years.'

'Can't help you Spiros. I've pleaded with her every day to go with you. What more can I do?' said Joe.

Sonia placed a bottle of Mythos on the bar with a chilled glass.

'Ef-hari-sto Sonia. And one for Joe!'

'Oh. Sorry Spiros. I'm going to Corfu Town. Supplies.'

Spiros suddenly became serious. 'Please Joe. I've had the day from hell.' He grabbed his forearm.

Joe looked at Sonia. She didn't offer him a way out. 'Just one. Then I have to go.'

'Thank-you. Thank-you.'

They sat together on high stools by the bar looking back across the canopied terrace towards the main street, which Joe had lined with garish signs advertising 'all day English breakfast, 150 drachmas' and 'Sunday roast 250 drachmas' along with the cost of popular brands of beer by the pint.

Spiros stared sadly into his beer for almost a minute before looking up at Joe. 'She's kicked me out.'

Joe couldn't even pretend to be surprised and wasn't even sure which woman Spiros was referring to. 'Your mistress or your wife?'

'Both.' Spiros looked back at his beer.

Joe was a little surprised now. He puffed his cheeks and blew a long sigh out through pursed lips. He lowered his head and looked up at Joe's sad face.

'Why?'

Spiros thought about it for a minute. He wasn't completely sure. He couldn't understand why any woman would leave him, even though he cheated on them all. He was good to them when he was with them. He turned back to Joe.

'Elaine told Clara I was sleeping with her.'

'Your mistress told your wife you were having an affair?'

Spiros nodded.

'So why is Elaine leaving you?'

'She found me in bed with Iokaste from the chip shop.' Spiros took a long swig of beer.

Joe also took a few gulps of beer. He had nothing to add which might help Spiros. He had plenty to say, but nothing positive. So he said nothing, but eventually couldn't resist.

'It was always going to happen.' He waited for a reaction, but nothing came. 'You can't live with two women in two houses and expect to get away with shagging around.'

'I know. I'm stupid.'

Joe couldn't help a little smile. 'But I have to admit, I didn't think you'd get away with it for this long.'

Spiros had moved in with Elaine White, a 25-year-old English holiday rep, the previous October having persuaded her to spend the off season with him in Corfu instead of going home for a few months. With countless empty holiday apartments available, she had secured a very cheap beach-side studio in Sidari.

Spiros had spent very little time with her as he needed to spend a lot of time looking after his 'sick mother', which was a lie. His mother was fit and well living in Athens. He had been spending most of his time with his wife Clara. She had been a 23-year-old English holiday rep when he met her ten years before. They now had three children and lived in the Corfiot village of Avliotes three miles south of Sidari on the hills high above the Ionian Sea, among the endless olive groves.

Clara had been so busy looking after their two boys, four and six, and two-year-old daughter that she had accepted his excessive working hours, which often took him on 'overnighters to the mainland'.

Unfortunately for Spiros, when Elaine found him in bed with Iokaste, she didn't confront him, but followed him back to the family home in Avliotes. She confronted the wife instead with Spiros as a hapless onlooker.

The sky had grown dark and the black clouds opened with a heavy shower, which cleared the air. Spiros finished his beer and sat listening to the water dripping off the canopy into a puddle on the terrace.

'The supplies can wait. Let's have another beer.' Joe opened another two bottles of Mythos.

'What next then Spiros?'

He shrugged his shoulders, pushed the chilled glass to one side and drank straight from the bottle.

'Dunno Joe. That's all happened today. Maybe it's in the stars. Maybe the worst is yet to come.'

They both saw Elaine at the same time walking across the terrace folding up her wet umbrella, turned to each other and nodded.

'Good luck Spiros.' Joe patted him on the back and left him to it.

'Hello arsehole. Thought I'd find you here. Probably been trying to get in Sonia's pants no doubt. We should have set off 15 minutes ago.' Elaine was the courier on Spiros' transfer trip to the airport.

'I was just waiting for the rain to stop babe.'

'Don't "babe" me you twat. The rain has stopped. Let's go.'

Spiros finished his beer and followed Elaine along the passage by the side of the bar, which led through to a large car park.

They said nothing more to each other as the bus stopped at a number of hotels in San Stefanos, Arillas and Agios Georgios before heading south towards Paleokastritsa where they would pick up the main road for Corfu town and the airport.

With a full load, the coach laboured up the steep inclines of the narrow road, which hugged the twisting contours of the hills that followed the rugged coastline of the island.

Elaine reached for the microphone. 'Good afternoon everybody. I hope you enjoyed your stay on the beautiful island of Corfu.' She added a little more about journey times, places they would pass through and details of their flight, but was more brief than usual and couldn't manage a smile. She sat back down and glared at Spiros from the fold-down single bench seat near the door.

He kept looking at her briefly out of the corner of his eye, unable to take his eyes off the road for long as the tight bends demanded a skilled driver, but her angry gaze was fixed on him. He could feel her disgust. They passed over the brow of the hill and started twisting down towards Paleokastritsa.

'Married with three kids,' Elaine blurted with venom.

Spiros had no reply.

'Better make that four.'

Spiros turned and faced her confused.

'I'm pregnant.'

3 ... **Two fingers**

Five months before the crash, Saturday, November 26, 1983: Giles Thornton knocked on the door of the referee's changing room and pushed it gently open without waiting for a reply.

'Hey big man. How the hell are you my friend?'

John Coyle had been preparing for a cup quarter-final between Southside YMCA and Ashtown Rovers. He used to play in the same team as Giles many years ago, but he was a referee now and Giles was the chairman of YMCA Football Club.

'Good mate. How 'bout you?' John stood and shook Giles' hand.

'Good. Very good. Business is booming and we've put a great side together. I think we can win this cup, but, obviously, we must win this game.' Giles frowned as he saw John wince a little. 'You okay? You don't look too good.'

John clasped his right hand with his left and rubbed gently. 'Well Giles. To be honest, I nearly went home. I've got a splitting headache and pains all over my body, like I'm being tortured on a rack. Worse thing is a stabbing pain in two fingers.'

'Some kind of flu?' Giles was concerned for his old friend.

'Don't think so. It started all of a sudden. One minute I was fine, then this.'

Giles was a tall black man, almost 40 and wore a dark suit with the club tie, but he was useless with health matters. 'Shall I get the trainer?'

'No. No. Don't worry. It'll pass. I've had a couple of aspirin.'

'You sure?'

'Yeah. Leave it. I've got bigger worries than a headache.'

Giles screwed his face up with sympathy. 'I did hear you'd missed out on a couple of contracts. And, sorry, I got the Wickstead job. I know you tendered, but I was already on site. Made sense for them really.'

They were both builders and times were hard, although Giles seemed to be picking up plenty of work.

John, on the other hand, was struggling badly and hadn't picked up any new jobs for almost a year, two contracts had gone unpaid as the other party had gone under and he had remortgaged his own house to try and keep things afloat. Worse than that, he had missed the last four payments and the mortgage company had been threatening repossession.

'Don't worry Giles. I had a tiny margin on my Wickstead quote anyway.'

That was a lie. The Wickstead job would have given him the leg-up he needed, but he didn't want Giles to feel bad.

'Tell you what Giles. I nearly joined the Fire Brigade. Thought a change of scenery might be a good idea.'

'Oh right. That's quite a big career change.'

'S'pose so. But I've always had this idea that if I could save one other person's life, I would deserve to live my own.'

'Bloody hell John. You always were a soppy fucker.' Giles shook him gently by the shoulder. 'What made you change your mind then?'

'Well. I didn't. I got as far as the interview and they didn't want me. It was tough getting that far though.'

Giles nodded approval.

'I wasn't sure I'd be fit enough, but I passed all the tests. Not bad for a slightly-overweight balding 46 year old.'

'You were one of the fittest players I knew. Never bloody stopped. Put me to shame.' Giles smiled. 'Was the pay any good?'

'Would have got me out of a hole.' John answered without thinking and immediately thought he had given too much away, but added nothing.

Giles was thoughtful for a moment, before stepping a little further into the room and shutting the door behind him. 'How bad is it?'

John didn't reply straight away. He looked down at his stopwatch and clicked the button a few times before looking up at Giles. 'We could lose our home.'

'Shit no,' exclaimed Giles. 'What does Sarah think?'

'She doesn't know. We're four months behind and she doesn't know a thing.'

John hadn't told his wife. He believed his happy marriage was built on her firm belief that he had all the answers and would always provide her and their two children with everything they needed all the time. Until now that had been true. He had built houses and traded property successfully and built up a tidy portfolio of rental units, but they had been slowly sold off to fund his building work and cover the losses on unpaid contracts.

'What you gonna do then?'

'Dunno Giles. Dunno.'

They were quiet for a moment.

'Tell you what John. I want to win this cup. You fix the game and I'll pay your mortgage arrears.' Giles kept a straight face.

John looked at him, not sure if he was serious. 'You are joking aren't you?'

'All your mortgage arrears. Fresh start.'

John was sure he was joking but was so desperate he almost wanted to believe it was a genuine offer.

'I know you're joking and you'll win anyway. You're way better than this side, especially with those two quality youngsters you have in the middle.'

'They're both on the bench. Punishment for not training.'

'Hmm. Could be close then, but no. I'd never do anything like that.'

A big smile spread across Giles' face. 'Course I'm joking. You're the most honest bloke I know.' Giles hugged his friend. 'And yes, we'll beat them anyway. But I might be able to push some work your way if you do me a favour.'

'Go on,' urged John.

'Have you heard about the plans to build 200 new homes in Southside?'

'Yeah. Everybody wants in on that.'

'Well, I'm pretty sure I have a big slice of the action, but I'm spread too thin. I could probably sub you some of the work.'

John shook his hand vigorously. 'Giles, you're a star.'

'But there's the favour I need.'

'Fire away.'

He edged a little closer. 'Have you ever been to Corfu?'

'Greek island isn't it?'

'That's right. Anyway, I've got a villa out there. Needs a bit of work. Haven't got the time myself and I don't trust my own staff to work on my place when I can't watch them closely.'

'You want me to go to Corfu?'

'Weeks work. That should be enough to put it straight. What do you think?'

'Expenses?'

'All expenses, all materials and double rate for the work.'

John raised his eyebrows. 'When?'

'Oh. No hurry. Some time after Christmas would be fine.'

John thought a little more before shaking Giles' hand again. 'Deal mate. You're on.'

'Excellent. Let's talk later. You have a good game. Cheers John.' Giles closed the door behind him and John sat down to do his laces.

'Aww,' he winced out loud. The pain in his fingers was sharp. Just two fingers on his right hand and he couldn't think what had caused it. The skin hadn't been broken. It felt as if they had been caught in a door jam, but nothing like that had happened.

He had a couple of minutes before he needed to start the game. His head was still throbbing and the aches in his body were not going away. His mind was in turmoil. He kept wondering whether Giles had been serious with his 'bung'. No chance. He wasn't that sort of bloke. Besides, he gave him a genuine offer. But then again, maybe that genuine offer was tied in to the result of the match.

As his thoughts consumed him, the tick of the clock above the referee's door seemed to grow louder and louder until it fell in line with the pulses of pain in his head and body. Tick, throb, tick, throb.

A shock win for the visitors would remove any doubt over Giles and his offer. John headed out to the centre circle and blew his whistle.

By half time the game had gone as John hoped. The underdogs were 2-1 ahead thanks to two penalties. Doubtless Giles would have a dig after the game.

Despite that, Giles' YMCA side had been the better team and they had a lot of quality on the bench. John knew it would probably still be a home win giving his big friend the result he wanted.

He sat on his own in the referee's room with a cup of tea. His thoughts were interrupted by a spasm of pain in his fingers. He heard a window smash in the distance and looked up at the clock, the tick louder than ever.

4 ... **Noisy young men**

Two hours before the crash, Wednesday, April 11, 1984: 'Here we go, here we go, here we go.' Marco, Twig, Rozzer, Dean and Len sang loudly as they clinked beer bottles together to toast their final drinking session in the Kavos Hotel. They were on a stag week in sleepy Arillas arranged by Marco's fiancée. They had expected a rowdy week in the Arillas Hotel in the bustling resort of Kavos, but Denise had tricked Marco into the deserted village of Arillas in the hope that he would face less temptation. The four young men, along with Marco's divorced father Len, had made their own entertainment in the hotel bar, much to the chagrin of the other few visitors.

Twig, a tall skinny ginger-haired 22-year-old postman, stood up a little too fast and his wicker chair fell back towards a pile of suitcases. 'Bus'll be here soon. Let's spoof to see who gets the last round.'

The others cheered their approval and fished around in their pockets for some coins.

An elderly couple in the neighbouring cluster of chairs collected their suitcases and headed for the relative calm of the terrace.

'Game on,' shouted the stag, Marco, as he thrust his clenched fist into the middle of the table.

Rozzer, Dean and Twig held out their fists.

'Come on you old fart.' Rozzer pushed Len gently. He had not been happy about Marco's father joining them for the stag week and didn't appreciate him slowing the game down.

Len held out his fist, reluctantly, now very tired of constant pressure from Rozzer to 'not be such a pussy'. He had joined the stag week against his better judgement after his future daughter-in-law had pleaded with him to watch over Marco. Len had commented at the time that such a lack of trust was hardly a firm foundation for a successful marriage. He added weight to his argument by telling her that his own marriage had failed partly due to a lack of mutual trust.

Nevertheless, he had made an effort 'not to be such a pussy' for the sake of Marco, but had been repeatedly tempted to punch Rozzer, a short man of Asian decent, who managed a betting shop on the high street in Croydon, opposite Marco and Denise's flat, quite a responsible job for a 23-year-old man, who had left school with very few qualifications.

'Seven,' shouted Marco.

'Six,' said Dean gently. He was a softly-spoken 22-year-old accountant, who had been through school with the others, and had always been happy to follow. He tried not to step out of line.

Marco was the dominant member of the group and thought Twig was taking too long. 'Come on Twig. Like you said, bus'll be here soon.'

'Eight.' Twig didn't like being hurried. He had all three coins hidden in his hand but didn't want to call too high in case he gave himself away.

'Nine,' said Len with confidence. He also had three coins in his clenched fist and had an idea that Twig had the same.

'Five.' Rozzer had an empty fist and planned on calling five before the round started and had stuck with it, even though he now thought it too low.

'Let's see what you got,' shouted Marco. He opened his fist to show no coins. Rozzer and Dean did the same followed by Twig and Len, each with three coins.

There was a loud cheer and Dean smiled modestly and raised both arms slightly above his head not wishing to celebrate too much for fear of gloating. Marco got him in a headlock and rubbed his knuckles in his mousy hair.

'Dean. You lucky bastard.' Marco pushed him back into his armchair. 'Game on lads.'

The remaining four fumbled with their coins and thrust their clenched fists over the table.

The noise level went up as the game reached a crescendo with Rozzer the last man out.

As the jeers died down, Rozzer sank into his seat with his face in his hands. Marco stood up next to him and pointed down at him theatrically while shouting across the empty room to the barman.

'Oi. Zorba. The drinks are on Rozzer. Five more bottles of Amstel.'

The barman nodded.

Marco got Rozzer in a headlock now. 'Rub his head Twig.'

The tall postman did as he was told. 'Come on Dean. You have a go,' urged Twig.

Dean shook his head. He didn't want to do it, but he struggled to know what to do. He didn't want to hurt Rozzer, but he didn't want to say 'no' to Twig.

'Get in there,' shouted Marco, and Dean quickly reached over and rubbed Rozzer's head gently with his knuckles.

Rozzer shook himself free and grunted as he reached for his wallet. He had been hoping to save the last of his cash for some food at the airport.

The barman walked past them with a tray of cocktails and headed out to the terrace.

Len followed him with his eyes before looking immediately back to the bar on the far side of the room. He took a double take and shook his head with surprise. The barman was behind the bar taking the lids off five bottles of beer.

How could he be in two places at the same time? Len stood and walked slowly over to the bar, sat on a tall stool and watched the barman as he opened a new pack of batteries, before reaching up to the clock behind the optics. He eased out the old batteries, but before putting in the new ones, he rested the clock against the till and turned to serve Len.

'Can I help you sir?'

Len turned and looked over his shoulder towards the terrace door, before looking back.

'I'm sure I just saw you go out that door and now you're behind the bar.'

'That's my twin brother Hypnos.'

A smile spread across Len's face.

The barman smiled.

'Now I can tell you're different.'

'How's that sir?'

'You just smiled.' Len held out his open hands and laughed softly, but the barman didn't share his amusement.

Len assumed he hadn't understood and tried to explain. 'Your brother hasn't smiled all week.' He spoke slowly. 'Seemed a bit unhappy.'

The barman raised his eyebrows and nodded gently. Then he leant towards Len and spoke quietly. 'You're lucky you didn't get my sister Keres.' The barman looked from one side of the room to the other, almost as if he were looking for Keres. 'She works here sometimes and a few years ago, she had a rowdy crowd, much the same as you have been this week.'

'Yeah sorry about that Zorba. We have been a bit loud.'

The barman withdrew slightly, a little irritated. 'My name is not Zorba.'

Len looked embarrassed. 'Sorry. Heard the others call you Zorba. Assumed they must have asked.'

'Your friends have not asked my name. They have only spoken to me when demanding more drinks.'

'I'm sorry. If I'd known…'

'No matter. It's done.'

'But it does matter. Please. What is your name?'

'Thanatos.'

Len held out his hand. 'Pleased to meet you Thantos. I'm Len.'

Thanatos shook his hand. 'Pleased to meet you too.' He paused briefly before adding, 'Thanatos. Not Thantos.'

'Thanatos,' repeated Len.

'You've got it.'

'Now Thanatos. Let me apologise properly for my friends. The bar's empty, you're not busy. Let me buy you a beer. Sit with us for a minute. Please.'

'I couldn't possibly.' He shook his head.

Len reached across the bar and rested his hand on the barman's shoulder. 'Please. I insist. We leave very soon. I would feel a lot better if you joined us. You'd be doing me a favour.'

Thanatos thought for a moment. 'Just one.' He grabbed another bottle and added it to the tray of beers.

'Excellent.' Len headed back to the others.

Thanatos served the beers before pulling up a chair next to Len and sitting down.

Marco held up his beer and welcomed their new friend. 'Hey Zorba. How's it goin' my son?'

Before he could answer, Len jumped in. 'Marco. It's not Zorba. His name is Thanatos.

Please,' he said with reverence. 'Have some respect for our hosts. We are guests in their country.'

It was water off a duck's back. 'Hey Thantos. How's it hangin' my little Greek friend?'

Without saying any more, Len pointed a warning finger towards his son, a gesture which had always worked when Marco was a child and still had some impact, but not as much as Len had hoped, so he pressed his argument. 'Marco.' He waited till he had his attention. 'Thanatos and his brother have been very patient with us. Show some manners.' He then turned to the young Greek barman. 'You were telling me how your sister Keres handled some rowdy guests.'

Len and his four young friends turned to Thanatos for his answer.

'She was patient at first.' He shrugged a little, almost apologising in advance for what he was about to tell them. 'But they got very drunk. All the other guests left and they couldn't keep their hands to themselves either.'

The boys waited patiently for Thanatos to continue.

'She gave them a free round of shots. There were three of them. "Down in one," they said, and moments later they all passed out. She had drugged them and before they came round, she drowned them. One at a time. In a bucket of beer.'

The boys were open mouthed until a hint of a smile appeared on the barman's face.

Marco burst out laughing. 'You had me going for a minute.'

'You bastard Zorba. You had me too,' added Rozzer.

'Thanatos,' replied Thanatos firmly.

'Nice one Thantos,' added Twig.

Len said nothing.

Dean wasn't sure how to react and went with the majority. 'You had me going too Thanatos.' He reached out his bottle. 'Cheers mate.'

'Okay lads. One last spoof.' Marco reached in his pocket for more change and handed Thanatos three coins. 'You in mate?'

'Okay. How do you play?'

'Dean.' Marco nodded at Dean and waved his head towards the barman.

'We each have three coins and put our fist forward containing none, one, two or three coins. We take it in turns to guess the total number of coins. When you get it right, you're out.'

'Last one in buys the beers?' asked Thanatos.

'You got it,' added Marco loudly. 'Game on.'

As they all fumbled for their coins, the barman thought for a moment. 'No time for more beer so what happens to the loser?'

'Good point,' Len nodded.

'True, true,' Rozzer agreed.

'What shall we play for then?' asked Thanatos.

'Money,' suggested Twig.

'I'm all out,' said Rozzer handing Thanatos his last note. 'Best give you this before I forget. Keep the change Zorba.'

'Thanatos.'

'Sorry. Thantos.'

'Dunno then,' said Marco. His friends were waiting for his leadership.

There was an awkward moment before Twig thrust out his clenched fist. 'Game on?' he asked.

The others followed suit, but not the barman.

'You in Thanatos?' asked Len.

'Do you mind if I make a suggestion?'

'Not if it's free beer,' shouted Rozzer.

The boys all cheered.

Thanatos waited for the noise to fall away. 'You are all about to get on the bus for the airport.'

'Yes,' nodded Marco.

The others nodded.

'Let's just suppose the bus crashes.'

'Blimey Zorba. You're a depressing fucker. First it was drowning in buckets of beer and now our bus crashes. Don't think I want to go on your stag night.'

'Let him finish.' Marco was curious now.

'Let's just suppose that only one of you can survive.'

'Okay,' nodded Marco. 'Four dead. One survivor. Okay.'

'Go on,' added Len.

'Let's spoof for the chance to live.' Thanatos waited for them to take in the idea.

Marco wasn't sure. 'Won't work.'

'Why not?'

'Because the last person in is supposed to be the loser.'

'Okay. Let's change things a bit. The last person in has to decide who lives. And it can't be themselves.'

Marco and Len looked at each other. 'Fair enough Dad? You okay with that?'

'Yeah. I'll do it.' He looked round at Thanatos. 'I love your dry wit. I wish we'd had a beer together earlier in the week.'

'Game on,' shouted Marco, thrusting his right fist forward as he swigged beer from the bottle in his free hand.

The others followed suit.

'You first,' Marco said to Thanatos. 'Anything from naught to eighteen.'

'None,' said Thanatos. No hint of a smile.

The others burst out laughing and swigged from their bottles.

After they all guessed, they opened their empty fists in turn. No coins. The barman's unlikely guess had been correct. Nobody laughed. Suddenly there was a feeling of sobriety and just a little apprehension, not because the barman had won the first round, but because he had been correct when everybody had thought his suggestion ludicrous.

Nobody said it, and nobody seriously thought it, but in the backs of their minds, the germ of an idea was forming. If Thanatos could confidently predict such an unlikely outcome in a game of spoof, maybe his suggestion that their bus would crash was not such a crazy idea.

Almost in unison, they drank from their bottles, and as they reached behind their backs and fumbled with the coins, their levels of concentration grew. Other thoughts entered their heads. Thoughts of pain. Thoughts of death. Thoughts of loved ones they may leave behind.

'Don't be so fucking stupid,' Marco whispered to himself under his breath. 'Game on,' he shouted and pushed his fist forward.

'Seven.' A safe call from Marco.

'Eight.' As safe as Dean could manage.

'Six.' Twig.

'Nine.' Len.

'Five.' Rozzer.

They all opened their fists. Nine. Len was out.

Marco looked over at his father. 'If I die and you live Dad, you'll have to marry Denise for me.' There was a ripple of nervous laughter around the table.

Twig and Rozzer went out next.

Marco and Dean put their hands behind their backs.

'Marco, you're my best mate,' said Rozzer. 'Pick me to live. I'll be a dad in two months. Helen can't survive without me.'

'She'll be better off without you Rozzer.' Twig was joking, but the atmosphere had soured.

'Fuck off Twig,' Rozzer snapped. 'Who needs another fucking postman? Best you die before me.'

'Hey. Calm down. It's a game. Just a game. Nobody's dying.' Marco held out his fist. 'Dean. Game on.'

Dean held out his fist.

Marco followed suit. 'One.'

'None,' said Dean.

Marco sighed deeply as he opened his empty hand knowing he had lost.

Dean opened his empty fist. 'Your shout Marco,' he said softly.

'Go on Marco. Who lives? Who dies?' Rozzer was impatient.

Marco sat back in his armchair and finished his beer.

'I've already thought about it.'

They all sat on the edge of their seats.

'Twig, Rozzer, Dean. We've been together since we all started at Croydon East Primary. We've played together, fought together, laughed together and drunk together. Dad I've known you a little longer and you're probably my best mate.' The others groaned. 'Sorry lads. He is though. But that's not why

I'm choosing him to survive. I'm choosing him because you three are my team. We lived together. We die together.'

'Thanks mate,' Twig liked the sentiment.

Dean patted him on the back. 'That's nice Marco.'

Rozzer finished his beer and looked towards the door. 'Where's the fucking bus?'

Len was genuinely moved and didn't know what to say. In a rare moment of unmanly weakness, he got up and hugged his son, while the barman collected the bottles and cleared them away.

Behind the bar, Thanatos put the new batteries in the clock and hung it back on the wall behind the optics.

'Bus is here,' shouted Twig.

They gathered their suitcases and headed for the door, but not before Marco and Dean shook Thanatos by the hand.

While they loaded their cases, Len thanked the barman and squeezed his shoulder. 'Sorry again. Bunch of heathens. Nice game though. Made 'em think a bit.'

'Ya-sou my friend. Take care.' Thanatos watched as the boys headed for the back seat.

Len shouted after them. 'I've got to stay at the front or I'll be sick. See you at the airport.'

5 ... **Hang on a minute**

Moment of impact, Wednesday, April 11, 1984: By the time Spiros Gekas had closed his mouth and looked back to where the bus was facing, he was on the wrong side of the road heading into a gentle bend at a dangerous speed. He only just made the bend, but the offside wheels were on the loose ground between the edge of the road and the crash barrier.

He jolted the steering wheel in an effort to get back on the road, but overdid it. As the front end of the bus whipped across to the far side of the road and started sliding on the wet surface, the back end of the bus started scraping against the corrugated metal crash railings before mounting them.

The front end twisted towards the wall on the inside of the bend and hit an olive tree, which sent the bus into a roll. After two and a half complete rolls, the bus slowed significantly, but continued to slide backwards on its roof towards the next sharp bend.

The impact with the barrier on the bend slowed the bus a little until it came to a halt half on the road and half over the edge of the cliff, a good 300 feet above the rocks that lined the top bay of Paleokastritsa.

Spiros was upside down, still in his seat, but the impact with the olive tree had pushed in the corner of the bus. Spiros was pinned in his chair by the steering wheel. The gear stick had also twisted towards him and was pressed firmly against the side of the seat. Spiros was trapped and suspended upside down.

Although restrained by the wreckage of ripped metal, he suffered no serious injuries, that he was aware of, and remained conscious. As he realised what had happened and started to focus on the new danger facing his passengers, he twisted his head to survey the damage.

'Elaine Babe. Elaine. Are you okay?' He shouted, frantically looking for her. Luggage, people and parts of the bus littered the inside of the vehicle. A mixture of smoke and steam filled the bus and there was an acrid smell of burning metal. Spiros assumed it had been caused by the steel roof of the bus sliding along the Tarmac.

As the air began to clear, Spiros caught a glimpse of what looked like Elaine's white dress. 'Elaine. Elaine. Is that you Babe?'

She didn't move and didn't reply. Spiros saw a man roll over on his back near the woman in white. 'Hey mister. You okay?'

Len rubbed his eyes. 'Yes. Good. How 'bout you?'

'Trapped but fine.' Spiros spoke fast with fear in his voice. 'Please mister. The girl in the white dress. The courier. Is she alive?'

'Hold on.' Len reached towards her. 'Ahh,' he yelled. 'I think I've broken my arm.'

'The girl?' Spiros was getting impatient. 'She's alive.'

'How bad is she?' shouted Spiros. He was struggling to hear Len for the screams of other passengers.

'Dunno. Okay I think,' shouted Len. He looked towards the back of the bus. The smoke was starting to clear and the noise had changed. The engine had cut out, but the radio was still playing a loop of British chart hits, but it was hard to hear above the groans and screams.

Len could now see clear sky through the smashed back window but swallowed hard when the tops of the hills on the other side of the bay came into view. He immediately thought of The Italian Job and was gripped with fear, but couldn't help a small smile as

the radio loop moved on to the next song …
My Name is Michael Caine by Madness. Len
expected it, but hoped there wouldn't be some
clown push himself forward and shout calmly,
'Hang on a minute. I've got a great idea.' He
certainly didn't have any himself and was torn
between self preservation and the burning
need to check on his son at the back of the
bus. He stayed where he was.

'Marco,' he shouted. 'Marco. You
okay?' He kept shouting, but nothing came
back from Marco or his three friends.

A plump man in his thirties was
suspended from the roof two thirds of the way
towards the back, his legs trapped between his
seat and the back of the seat in front. 'What's
he look like mate?' Geoff Miller shouted up
to Len.

'Red shirt.'

'There's a bloke down here in red. About
sixty. Is that him?'

'No. Early twenties. Back seat probably.'

Geoff contorted himself so he could look
towards the back seat. 'Fuck me,' he said
under his breath. There were a few people
near the back window. Geoff could make out
a ginger-haired man and somebody with a red
shirt, but there was no movement. They
looked as if they had been thrown from their

seats and probably killed instantly when the bus hit the crash barrier, back-end first.

Len shouted again. 'Anything? What can you see?'

Geoff had to concentrate hard to stay conscious. The pain in his legs was overwhelming, but he could see that passing out could cost his life, so he held on. They all needed to get off the bus quick. He didn't want to be shouting bad news, but he feared the man at the front may come looking if he didn't and that could tip the bus over the edge.

Geoff screwed his face up in anguish and shouted forward. 'Sorry mate. I can see a red shirt, but there's no movement. Doesn't look good.'

Len couldn't reply. He couldn't speak. He just lay still. Until he knew for sure, there was still hope.

The music moved on to The Snot Rap by Kenny Everett. Len could feel tears welling up in his eyes, but the irony of such a bizarre song filling the wreckage of their bus made him laugh.

A creak of metal echoed around the coach as it tipped a little further. Fresh screams filled the air and Len snapped out of his trance to try the door. He stepped carefully over the girl in white and reached up to the handle. There was no movement. Looking through the door, Len could see rocks and vegetation up against the side of the bus. Even if the door would move, there were too many obstructions. There was no way out through the door. Some windows were shattered, but the windscreen was intact. Only the back window had smashed and gone, leaving everyone with a clear view of sky and the hills around Paleokastritsa.

'The door's jammed,' shouted Len. 'Better all keep still and wait for help.'

'The side door might be okay,' shouted Geoff.

Gordon Teal, who had been nursing his unconscious wife, rested Mary's head against her hand luggage and reached for the handle of the second door. It swung open. 'Woahh,' shouted Gordon. 'It's open, but it's over the edge of the cliff. No way out here.' He saw a huddle of three children crying and holding onto each other between two suitcases near the open door. 'You keep still kids. Stay well away from that door okay?'

The eldest child, about eight, nodded and reached his arms around his younger brother and sister.

The air had cleared, the smell of burning metal was still strong, but the dominant sound was now sobbing and groans of pain, with the quiet tinkle of the radio in the background, now playing Moonlight Shadow by Mike Oldfield.

Another creak of metal sent a panic around the bus as it tipped a little more over the cliff.

Roy Farrell and his wife Daisy, both aged 52, had survived the impact largely unhurt, but the fear of what may happen next left Daisy short of breath. She tried to take deep breaths, but couldn't.

'Where's your bag?' Roy shouted with great urgency.

She shook her head unable to speak.

Roy shouted down the bus. 'Black linen bag. Anybody seen it? Wooden handles.'

There was no reply.

'Please,' repeated Roy. 'My wife needs her inhaler. She's having an asthma attack. Black bag.'

Again there was nothing. Roy started rifling through the debris as Daisy started wheezing.

Geoff Miller, still conscious, but starting to lose all feeling in both legs, in some respects preferable to the intense pain, twisted his head from his upside down position to look for the lost bag. There was nothing in the mess spread across the ceiling, which now formed the floor. As he looked back up to the seats, he caught a glimpse of the wooden handles. 'I think I see the bag.'

'Can you throw it up the bus?' asked Roy with enormous relief.

Geoff stretched, but couldn't get near the bag. 'Sorry mate. Can't reach it.'

'Please,' screamed Roy, desperate again.

'Sorry mate. I'm trapped.'

Roy started stepping over bodies and luggage as he worked his way towards the back of the bus.

'No,' shouted about 15 passengers, almost as one.

'You'll tip us off the cliff you idiot,' shouted Geoff, but Roy was determined. He climbed over a loose pair of chairs and as he stepped towards the open side door, there was a loud creak and the bus tipped a little more. Roy stopped, but the creaking carried on for a couple more seconds until the bus came to rest again. The passengers looked out of the back window with horror as they saw the sea for the first time.

Roy gave up on the bag and slowly climbed back over the loose pair of seats. He edged closer to Daisy and the creaking started again. The bus swayed back towards safety and a small ripple of applause filled the bus.

Geoff didn't want anybody taking any more chances. 'Don't anybody move.'

The shock of almost falling off the cliff rendered his comment utterly unnecessary. It was clear to everyone that they had to keep still if they wanted to live.

But Geoff couldn't resist the temptation. 'Hang on a minute. I've got a great idea.'

6 ... **A fiver says I can**

Ten years before the crash, Tuesday, April 23, 1974: 'A fiver says I can.' Geoff Miller couldn't resist a gamble.

'I shouldn't, but yes. I'll take your money off you. There's no way you'll finish that wall with what you have left in that tin.' Costa had been Geoff's partner in their decorating business since they both left school nearly ten years ago.

'Watch and learn Costa.' They shook hands.

Geoff poured the rest of the paint into his tray and started rolling. It was a large wall in a large house ... a big country manor a few miles west of Dorking. There was only about seven feet of wall left to do, but the wall was about ten feet tall. Costa had done the cutting in and Geoff just had to fill what was left with thick creamy magnolia emulsion.

'Thinned bottom coat, you'd have done it Geoff, but this stuff is going on thick.'

'We shall see,' smiled Geoff as he nodded his head to Seasons In The Sun by Terry Jacks, which was playing on Radio One.

'We had joy, we had fun, I bet Costa and I won,' sang Geoff as he closed in on the last two feet.

'But the fun didn't last, 'cause the paint ran out too fast,' sang Costa.

With two widths of his roller left to do, Geoff started scraping around the tin with a cement trowel to get the last few dregs. With one width of the roller left to do, the tin was empty, the tray was empty and Geoff started running his roller over the wet paint on the wall to try and spread it a little further, but it was no use. He fell short by one roller width over half the height of the wall. 'Fuck it Costa.'

Geoff started a new tin and finished the wall before sitting down in the corner and opening his lunch box.

Costa sat next to him. 'You'll never bloody learn will you.'

'So close though. You can't say I was wrong.'

'Okay Geoff. You were unlucky. But you're always unlucky.'

'No I'm not. I inherited a house.'

'Geoff. That wasn't lucky. Your father died of cancer at 46. Your ma left him when you were ten and the only reason you didn't have to share the house with four siblings was because your ma miscarried four times.'

'Okay Costa. Four miscarriages was quite unlucky, but that was my mum. Not me. The house was a lucky break. You can't tie it in with my dad and call it unlucky.'

'Okay. I won't, but how long was it before you had to mortgage the place to pay off your gambling debts?'

'Yes. I had a bad spell, but I had a couple of big wins before that.'

'And you lost the lot.'

Geoff thought for a minute. He didn't like to think of himself as unlucky, but needed examples. 'It was only a small mortgage.'

'Not the point Geoff. You owned that house in full and you had to pawn it to a building society to cover your losses. No wonder Kez left you.'

'Ahh,' said Geoff realising he had a winning argument. 'But she came back six months later.' He nodded triumphantly. 'And she cleared the mortgage for me.'

'Geoff. Your wife's grandma dies and she uses her money to clear your debts. Tell me how that makes you lucky.' Costa took a bite of his sandwich. 'Mind you, the fact that such a nice girl like Kez came back to a no-hoper like you surprised me. I thought you had no chance. So maybe you were lucky.'

Geoff smiled. He was happy with that. They tucked in to their lunch while You Won't Find Another Fool Like Me by The New Seekers played in the background.

'I bloody hope not. One's enough.'

'One what?' asked Geoff.

Before Costa could explain, the owner of the house came in with a silver tray full of fine China and biscuits.

'Think you deserve a break boys,' said Ronald Thornton-Groom as he pulled up a chair and placed the tray on an upturned milk crate near the pots of paint.

'Thank-you very much,' said Geoff, smiling at Costa. 'I was just thinking a cup of tea would be lovely and you walked in Mr Thornton.'

'That was lucky Geoff,' Costa conceded.

'Lovely place you've got here Mr Thornton.' It was the sort of place Geoff would buy Kez if any of his big bets ever came good. He'd need a massive win on the Pools though for a place this big.

'Thank-you young man. Costs a small fortune to keep it going though.'

'Maybe you could move to a smaller place,' suggested Costa.

'Oh no. I don't think so.' Ronald didn't like that idea. 'Fortunately we have a small fortune, so we're okay.'

'Oh right.' Costa struggled to get his finger through the handle of the tea cup. He gave in and lifted the cup with his hand underneath.

'Besides, we need all the land for our horses.'

'How much land?' asked Geoff.

Ronald thought for a moment, rubbing his right ear lobe. 'I'd say about…' He thought some more. 'About 120 acres.'

'Blimey,' exclaimed Costa.

'How many horses?' Geoff couldn't help asking.

Ronald rubbed his right ear lobe a little more. 'Twenty or so.'

Costa and Geoff looked at each other and both raised their eyebrows.

'Blimey,' exclaimed Costa again.

Geoff took a bite of his banana. 'I heard you only need one acre per horse.'

Ronald laughed. 'We don't need the grass to feed them. We need the space to train them. We need the gallops.'

'Race horses?' asked Costa.

Ronald nodded.

'How are your results going?' Geoff was starting to think he may be on to something.

'Not bad. We've had four wins this season, five seconds and eight thirds.'

'Doesn't seem much from 20 horses.' Costa wasn't impressed.

'Oh. We don't race them all. Some are for breeding and some are too young to race.'

Costa smiled acknowledgement.

'Besides, we've done better than last year, and ...' He looked around as if he were checking to see if anyone were listening. 'And we will do better next year.' He tapped his nose with his forefinger.

'Next year?' asked Geoff.

Ronald beckoned them a little closer. 'I have two horses coming through that will sweep the board. Wow. They can move. I think they'll win the lot and make me very wealthy.'

'You're already very wealthy,' Costa couldn't help pointing out.

'Wealthier,' Ronald assured them.

'What are they called?' asked Geoff.

'Yellow Submarine and Eight Days A Week.'

'Worth a bet then?' asked Geoff.

'Certainly young man. You could bet your house on them,' Ronald smiled.

'He was joking,' Costa could see through Geoff's glazed expression.

'I know. I know.'

'Best leave you to it boys.' Ronald collected the cups and left.

'Don't even think about it Geoff.' Costa could read his partner like a book and knew he was working out how to raise money. 'He could be wrong. Horses are a mug's game. Anything can happen.'

'Give me some credit Costa. I told you. I know he was joking and I don't bet on horses. I'm not stupid. Just unlucky.'

'Oh right. We're getting somewhere then.'

'What next?'

Costa picked up five rolls of wallpaper and looked towards the end wall. 'Think that should do it.'

'You won't need that many.'

Costa looked surprised. 'At least five rolls. Maybe six.'

'Four. Easy. With spare.' Geoff was adamant.

Costa started mixing the paste. 'Don't forget, you always lose a bit in off-cuts.'

'I know.' Geoff opened up the wallpaper table and prepared the equipment. 'Tell you what Costa. Give me a chance to get my fiver back.'

Costa laughed.

'Double or quits. I can do that wall with four rolls.'

'I shouldn't, but I can't help myself. That's something you should understand. I'll take your money off you. There's no way you'll finish that wall with four rolls.'

They shook hands.

Geoff started papering and nodded his head to Blockbuster by The Sweet. 'Does anyone know the way? There's got to be a way. To wallpaper,' sang Geoff, full of confidence.

'You just haven't got a clue what to do,' sang Costa.

'We shall see. We shall see.' Geoff was still confident. Climbing the step-ladders left him a little out of breath though. He was a portly young man, mid twenties, but didn't do enough exercise to burn off all the food he ate, but apart from an oversize tummy, he was in good shape, so he couldn't understand why his legs were getting sore, both in the same place, just below the knee.

With three rolls gone, Geoff was about three quarters of the way across the wall. 'Looking good my friend.'

Costa shook his head. 'Looking good for me. Not you.'

Geoff had been so careful to avoid waste that by the time he started pasting the last piece of paper, it was long enough to go from top to bottom of the wall and it looked about the right width.

Geoff enjoyed the thrill of a bet and as he neared the end of the wall, he could feel the tension build. He could almost hear his watch ticking towards the climax, which was odd, because it was digital. He lifted the paper and held it to the wall. There was a gap of just over an inch left at the end. 'Fuck it Costa.'

7 ... **'I don't like secrets'**

Moments after the crash, Wednesday, April 11, 1984: Daisy Farrell was a fit 52-year-old apart from her asthma. She gasped for breath as her husband Roy struggled towards the back of the bus to find her inhaler. She was sat upright on the ceiling of the coach, wedged between a suitcase and a large balding man, who had not moved since the bus came to rest on the cliff-top.

'How are you feeling Mrs Farrell? Can I get you another pillow?'

Daisy's breathing was suddenly normal. She sat up in her hospital bed so she could follow Roy's progress down the bus, but he had stopped. Everybody had stopped. It was silent apart from a nurse at the end of Daisy's bed, who was adjusting her lapel watch.

'I know you don't I?'

'You may recognise me.'

Daisy waited for her thoughts to clear. 'Yes I do know you. You delivered my baby 26 years ago.'

The Grim Reaper raised her eyebrows in encouragement.

'That's right.' It was all coming back to Daisy. 'You were the midwife at Southside Hospital. Delivery room six. I do know your name. Just remind me.'

'I'm the Grim Reaper.'

'No you're not.'

'Yes I am.'

'You're my midwife. I just told you.'

'Daisy. I am … I assure you … the Grim Reaper. You choose what I look like.'

'Where's your cloak and scythe?'

'I could have them if you want.'

'Okay I do. If you've come for me, I want to be sure you are who you say you are.'

Grim shrugged her shoulders. 'Okay. Click your fingers.'

Daisy clicked her fingers and immediately wished she hadn't. Grim instantly appeared in cliché Hollywood movie mode; a black faceless hooded blend of dirty grey smoke and solid matter screaming over her head with a huge scythe poised to strike.

She recoiled in horror and clicked her fingers.

The midwife sat quietly on the end of her bed. 'Are you ready to talk to me?'

Unable to speak for a moment, Daisy nodded slowly, but thought quickly. She couldn't understand why she had not been taken by the Grim Reaper already. And she couldn't understand why she had a choice in the Grim Reaper's appearance. If she could choose what Grim looked like, maybe she had other choices. Maybe she could avoid death if she chose well.

'Why can I choose what you look like?'

'Well. That's a hard one to answer. You don't actually choose, but you play a big part in my appearance. I know a lot about you. And you have spent the last 27 years burdened with guilt. The guilt has shaped you. It is such a big part of you that when I saw you for the first time, your guilt was the first thing that struck me.'

'That sounds pretty straightforward to me. You said it was a hard one to answer.'

'I did. Yes. But you're guilt only partly decides my appearance.'

'What else does?'

'My whims.' Grim leaned back on the bed and took a deep breath. 'And my whims change all the time.' Grim looked around the silent bus before turning back to Daisy. 'But some things never change.' She sat up again and faced Daisy. 'I don't like secrets.'

Grim followed the change in Daisy's expression. She could see realisation dawning slowly in her mind. 'That man down the bus is risking his life, and the lives of everybody on the bus, to save you.'

Daisy nodded.

'He has devoted his whole life to you and your son.'

She nodded again.

'It's not even his son and you've let him believe it is for 26 years. That's a big secret. A lot of guilt. You told Roy you'd never have a second child. "Too much pain," you said. "We're adopting if you want another," you said. So you let him bring up another man's son as his own and never gave him a chance to have his own child.'

'He was happy. He didn't need to know,' Daisy snapped back. 'Yes. I made a mistake. I had an affair, but it was over. Roy wanted the baby as much as I did. He didn't need to know. The burden of guilt was mine. Not his. He's had it easy compared to me.'

Grim didn't like that. 'I see. So you've done him a favour.' Grim looked at her with raised eyebrows. 'I think I feel one of my whims coming on.'

'What do you want then? Am I dying or not? Why are you here?' Daisy couldn't hide her anger and didn't like being preached to, by a midwife she hadn't seen for decades.

'I have a quota to fill. There are 50 souls on the bus, I must take 16.'

Daisy smiled. 'Not so clever after all. The rep told me there were only 47 passengers, plus her and the driver. Still one short of your 50.'

'There are 50 souls on the bus,' Grim repeated with quiet assurance.

'Okay. Whatever you say Mrs Reaper. Do I die or not?'

'That question may help me make up my mind.' Grim looked at Daisy with disappointment in her eyes. 'Don't you want to know if Roy will die?'

'Course I do. I would have asked that next.'

'Yes. I'm sure you would,' replied Grim with thinly disguised disdain.

'Well,' pressed Daisy impatiently.

'One of you must die.'

'Me or Roy?'

'Yes.'

'Who then?'

Grim didn't like being pushed and had grown to dislike Daisy very quickly. 'There is another couple on this bus in a similar situation. One of them must die. I have already spoken to them both.'

'What happened?'

'I told them they could make the choice.'

'So me and Roy can choose?' Daisy smiled.

'No.'

The smile turned to a scowl. 'Why not?'

'Because you always get your own way and you would willingly allow Roy to die.'

'You don't know that.'

'Oh, but I do.'

'How?' Daisy's voice went up an octave.

'I can read your thoughts.'

Daisy waited briefly. She doubted that were true. 'Go on then. What was the first thing that came into my head after you said you could read my thoughts?'

'First thing?'

'Yeah.'

'There was a small pause. No thought at all for a couple of seconds.'

'And next?'

'"That's me fucked then."'

'Shit. Why are we still talking? You can see what a selfish bitch I am.'

'A lot of people have some very selfish thoughts which they never actually say to other people. You're not unusual in that. I won't condemn you for it. In fact it's refreshingly honest of you to recognise your weakness, albeit a little late in the day.'

'So if it's not unusual to be as selfish as I am, why won't you let me and Roy decide between us who dies?'

'Because Roy is one of those rare people who not only doesn't say unkind things, he doesn't even think them. He wouldn't stand a chance. On top of which, your conscious thoughts are a thin veneer over your genuine subconscious feelings. And that veneer is often a shade more brazen than your true thoughts. Both men and women have a tendency to try and be a little more macho than they really are, even in the privacy of their own mind. Deep down the reality is often very different. So different in your case that I'm not prepared to let you and Roy decide which of you dies.'

'So you're actually saying I'm nicer than I think I am?'

'Yes.'

Daisy smiled. 'I like that.'

'But you totally lack integrity, so your good qualities rarely make an appearance.'

Daisy's smile melted away once more. 'So what happens if I don't get my inhaler?'

'That's up to me. If you pass out, you will die, but, although the stress of the crash has amplified the effects of the asthma attack, that was not the initial cause. The fumes triggered the attack and they are slowly clearing, so you may recover without your inhaler.'

'So the level of stress pushes me one way or the other?'

'That's right.'

'And you set the stress level?'

'Pretty much.'

'What's your choice then?'

'Ahh. Haven't made it yet. Got to speak to Roy first.' With that, Grim reached for her lapel watch.

Daisy struggled for breath as the shouting and sobbing once again filled the bus with Mike Oldfield's Moonlight Shadow tripping along in the background.

8 ... **The 50th soul**

Six months before the crash, Tuesday, October 4, 1983: 'Sonia. I'll have one more cocktail of the day before Spiros gets here.' Elaine White, wearing a short peach summer dress and a beaming smile, was in Joe's British Pub waiting for her Greek boyfriend to drive her to the airport. She was booked on a flight home to England after a summer as a holiday rep in Sidari.

Sonia, who ran Joe's bar with husband Joe, had become good friends with Elaine having hosted her welcome meetings. She shared a drink with Elaine ahead of her return home and was delighted her friend was leaving. She would miss her enormously, but Sonia knew more about Elaine's Greek boyfriend than Elaine did.

He already had three children and a wife, but loved to play the field, especially when the field was so full of bubbly, enthusiastic, young ladies from Britain either working temporarily or over on holiday with fun as their top priority.

Sonia was also good friends with Spiros Gekas, the Greek boyfriend, so her loyalties were split. Elaine's return to England was the best way forward for all, but Sonia's hopes were about to be dashed.

'I've had such a good time in Corfu and Spiros is so sweet.' Elaine couldn't stop smiling.

'Well he's certainly put a spring in your step. Can't deny that.'

'You're not really that keen on him are you?'

Sonia rolled her eyes.

'Why not Sonia?'

'Elaine. You know what I think. I've told you a thousand times. You know I like him. I love him to bits, but I wouldn't trust him as far as I could kick him.'

'But you don't know him like I do.'

'Elaine.' Sonia paused, making sure she had Elaine's full attention. 'He's in here every night and he chats up every girl who looks remotely interested. And those that aren't, he still undresses them with his eyes. He's insatiable.' Sonia wanted to add, 'And he's married with three kids,' but she knew Elaine would be devastated, so she hoped to prize them apart with more subtle encouragement.

'I know he's a charmer, but it's just a front. I love him and he tells me he loves me all the time.'

'He tells you what you want to hear.'

Elaine's smile briefly faltered. 'You're such a cynic. You can't see the good in people.'

Sonia sighed. She knew she was swimming against the tide.

'Listen to this.' Elaine edged forward. 'He picked me up at noon and drove me to Peroulades, bought me lunch at Seventh Heaven, table on the cliff edge, sun dancing on the sea below, mountains of Albania in the background. Then he bought a bottle of champagne and we took it down to the beach, hardly anyone else there. We drank and paddled in the sea and then he asked me.'

Sonia closed her eyes in despair. 'Go on. What did he ask you?'

Elaine's beaming smile was back. 'He asked me to move in with him over winter instead of going home.'

Sonia couldn't hide a look of complete shock.

Elaine assumed Sonia was shocked by how committed Spiros had been.

Sonia's shock was for completely different reasons and she had trouble getting an image out of her head, which included Elaine playing with Spiros' kids and sharing the household chores with his wife Clara. 'Have you seen his house?'

'I've never actually been there.'

'And why do you think that is?'

'I'm not sure I like your tone Sonia. What are you trying to say? It's no secret. He's doing his place up and there's no water or electricity.'

'Oh I see,' Sonia said with as much sincerity as she could muster. 'So you wouldn't mind living in a house with no power and water through the winter. It can be just as cold as England you know.'

'Wouldn't be a problem. With the tourists all gone, I could get an apartment for next to nothing here in Sidari.'

'And Spiros would share it with you?'

'Yes.' Elaine's smile had gone. 'Why can't you be happy for me?'

Sonia did her best. 'Elaine I am.' She gave her a hug. 'What are you goin' to do then?'

'Said I'd think about it. Tell him today when he picks me up.'

Sonia tried not to react, but gently shook her head. She couldn't help it.

'What's the matter with you? I thought you were my friend.'

'I'm sure things will go well.' The forced sincerity was transparent. She tried harder. 'You know I've got my doubts about Spiros, but he is, without doubt, thoroughly charming and I know he'll be the perfect gent.' But Sonia knew he would also be the perfect gent to his wife and any other girl that caught his eye. She prepared another couple of cocktails.

'You worry me sometimes Sonia. You can be so negative. I'm 25 now, nearer 30 than 20. I don't want to die a lonely old spinster. I think Spiros could be the one. I can see us getting married, nice little villa, couple of kids.' Elaine stared aimlessly into the distance as she day-dreamed.

Sonia closed her eyes and rested her face in her hands.

Elaine was a little put out by Sonia's lack of faith in Spiros. She felt insulted. 'Okay. So Spiros has an eye for the ladies. He's a good looking man. Why shouldn't he, as long as it goes no further than looking?

Your Joe's no different. He always talks to my chest instead of my face and charming the lady customers is part of his job. He does it well and you don't criticise him. Why's he any different to Spiros?'

Sonia knew she was on dangerous ground now. Without mentioning Spiros' wife and the countless girls she had seen him groping in the bar, she had very little to defend her own husband, although she was quite confident that Joe was all talk and no action, whereas Spiros was lots of talk and even more action.

Sonia had no answer and Elaine pressed her advantage. 'Tell you what Sonia. Let's test your confidence in Joe.'

Sonia nodded.

'Let's just suppose Joe was on his own in the bar and it was nearly closing time. Three or four in the morning. Something like that and the only customers left are a hen party of girls in their early 20s. All drunk. Laughing and joking and flirting with your Joe.'

'Okay.'

'There's 12 girls and they offer Joe an extra 10,000 drachmas, thirty quid or so, to serve their drinks topless. Would he do it and would he only be thinking about the extra profits?'

Sonia thought for a moment. 'Yes he'd do it and he would be thinking about the extra profits.'

'Only the extra profits?' Elaine asked swiftly.

'No. I hadn't finished. He would be thinking about the extra profits, but he'd probably enjoy doing it as well.'

'Okay, let's suppose they finish that round and order another. This time they offer him 20,000 drachmas if he serves them wearing only his pants.'

Sonia sighed. 'Yeah. I think he'd still take the money.'

'Now we're getting somewhere. Naked 40,000?'

'No. Absolutely not.' Sonia didn't have to think about that one.

'How can you be so sure?'

'I just am. I know my Joe.'

'And I know my Spiros. In the same situation, I don't think he'd have taken the 20,000. Maybe topless but nothing more.'

'Elaine, he'd have paid them 40,000 and carried their cocktail jug out suspended on the end of his erect penis.' Sonia held up her hands in apology. 'Only joking. I'm sure your right.'

Elaine half smiled. 'If you weren't such a good friend, I could take offence at that.'

Sonia prepared two more cocktails, handed Elaine her Sex On The Beach and sat back at the table.

'Elaine. My turn.'

'Okay. Shoot.'

'Right. I want you to close your eyes for this one.'

'Why?'

'I want you to have a really clear picture in your head.'

'Okay.'

'It is six months from now. You have spent the winter in Sidari and seen very little of Spiros. He has told you his mother is ill and needs him at her bedside. You catch him shagging Iokaste from the chip shop. In a rage, you follow him to Avliotes where you discover he has a wife and three children. You dump him but have to do an airport run later that day on his coach. During the trip you tell him you are pregnant. He is so shocked he crashes the bus. It rolls and slides half off the cliff above Paleokastritsa upside down but doesn't fall.'

'Bloody hell Sonia. I have a very clear picture in my head. It's not nice.'

'You are alive but unconscious. Spiros is alive and conscious but trapped in his seat, which could be a problem because the coach may fall off the cliff.'

'I don't like this Sonia. It almost feels real.'

'Keep your eyes shut. I then appear as the Grim Reaper and talk to you.'

'What do you say?'

'There are 50 souls on this bus. I must take 16.'

'Have you come for me?'

'No. You have a bad bump on the head and a few bruises, but you'll come round in a minute. You'll be fine.'

Elaine breathed a sigh of relief. 'So my baby's fine as well then?'

'Not necessarily.'

'Why not? You said I live.' Elaine's joy was short lived.

'Your unborn baby is the 50th soul.'

'But surely he's part of me and counts less?'

'From the moment of conception until the day I come for you, whatever age, race, religion or sex, every soul is counted equally by my boss when he sets his quota for each job.'

Elaine's lip quivered as she shed a tear. 'So what happens to my baby?'

'You must make a choice. I must take one life from either your unborn baby or his father Spiros.'

Elaine shuddered. 'I can't do that. I'm not prepared to do it.'

'You have to do it. You have 30 seconds to choose. If you don't, I'll take them both.'

'You can't do that.'

'I'm the Grim Reaper. I can do pretty much what I like. Who do you want to save? Twenty seconds.'

'I can't save just one.' Elaine spoke fast. 'You're making me kill one. Spiros has three children to support and I have always dreamt of having my own child, even if the father is no good.'

'Twelve seconds.'

'I hate Spiros, but I still love him. I love my own child already and I've only known I'm pregnant for six days.' Elaine's voice was frantic.

'Six seconds.'

'Sonia. No.'

'Three seconds.'

Elaine burst into tears as she shouted, 'Take the baby.'

9 ... **Sleeping tramp**

Three years before the crash, Saturday, July 25, 1981: 'So Mr Coyle, tell us why you want to volunteer for Oxfam's Overseas Emergency Relief teams.'

'I want to save lives.'

The Oxfam interview panel of six nodded approval.

'The only contribution I make to the community at the moment is being a football referee. I want to do more.' John had their attention. 'I believe that if I can save at least one other life, I deserve to live my own, and helping with disaster relief overseas will give me that opportunity.'

The panel chairman was not convinced. 'That's an admirable ambition Mr Coyle, but how does somebody with such ideals become a property developer?'

John tried to hide his disappointment. Oxfam generally chose candidates from the emergency services and he could see his commercial background was going to be a problem. 'Not all property developers are rich and blinkered to the needs of those around them. I'm actually going through a quiet spell at the moment, temporary I hope, but helping others is important to me.'

The chairman nodded without expression and turned to his colleagues. 'Any more questions?'

They shook their heads.

'Okay, I think we're ready for your presentation now.'

John had been asked to do a brief talk on any subject loosely related to working in a foreign country following an earthquake or other natural disaster. The subject, he had been told, was not too important as they were more keen on seeing how he delivered his message.

John stood up. 'Having spoken to some of your current disaster workers, I feared you may be wary of my background and question my motives for being here. I know you are worried about attracting wealthy adventurers looking for adrenalin-charged action holidays. I'm not one of those. I have a successful business, but that's because I work hard and apply my skills well, so the theme of my talk is … don't jump to conclusions.'

The panel chairman raised one finger. 'How does this relate to helping earthquake victims?'

John was ready for that one. 'When you are faced with a dangerous situation and desperate people, a clear head is vital. Snap judgements based on prejudice and cliché could prove costly. You must think clearly and take an impartial view.'

He lowered his finger. 'Okay. Carry on.'

'When I was a child, my grandmother Marion was secretary of Southside North Women's Institute. She ran the group with clockwork efficiency. In fact she did everything with clockwork efficiency, partly because it made life easier and partly because she liked everybody to know where they were up to. It avoided problems. She didn't like arguments. She always avoided conflict of any kind.

'She once told me about a train journey to London. She used to meet her sister once a month, always the second Monday, have some lunch and shop for clothes. She always took a five pound note. That was a lot of money back then.'

A couple of panel members smiled, but still no expression from the chairman.

'She told me once, during the train journey into London, she had a compartment to herself, but was joined at the next stop by a very scruffy and smelly old lady. She had a length of string around her waist to keep her raincoat snug. She had a black boot on one foot and brown shoe on the other. All her stuff was in a carrier bag. She smiled at my grandmother and settled in the seat at the far corner.

'Marion felt uneasy, but she was exhausted from a run of late nights and soon fell asleep. The train jolted as it pulled away from the next station and she woke up. She looked at the scruffy woman before checking her handbag hadn't been touched. The tramp had fallen asleep and Marion's bag was where it should be. Just to be sure, my grandmother opened her purse. She took a sharp intake of breath as she noticed the five pound note had gone.'

John noticed a look of curiosity on the faces of the panel members, even the chairman. 'She didn't know what to do. Should she seek help from a member of staff or confront the scruffy lady? Neither choice was attractive, especially as she didn't want trouble. If she could get the money back without waking the old woman, that would be best. She could see the tramp was desperate and forgave her, but she needed the money back.

'She quietly edged towards the woman's carrier bag and gently opened it up. There was the five pound note tucked under a clear plastic waterproof mac. She reached in slowly and pulled it out. Back in her own seat, she stayed awake for the rest of the journey before meeting her sister for lunch and shopping for a new head scarf.

'When she arrived home, my grandfather admired the scarf and asked if Marion's sister had leant her the money to buy it. "No," replied my grandmother. "I only ask," said my grandfather, "because you left your five pound note on the kitchen table."

'Marion was appalled that she had made such a mistake. Five pounds to the tramp would have been a fortune and she warned me that I must never make assumptions about anybody or anything.'

There was a ripple of approval from the panel.

'Ooh,' winced John.

'You okay?' asked a young lady on the panel with genuine concern.

'Thanks. I think so,' replied John. 'I just had a sharp pain in my hand. No matter. It's gone now.'

'Are you done?' asked the chairman of the panel with a blank face, giving nothing away. John could see he had made very little impact on the man, a feeling which would be confirmed two weeks later with a letter of rejection. Still, he battled on.

'Almost finished. So, in conclusion, don't jump to conclusions was my theme and just as we travel to places all round the world where we must keep an open mind to the people and situations that we find, I think we should always be wary that we will be judged on our arrival.

'With that in mind, we must be cautious and as neutral as possible in our appearance so that we are judged on what we say and do, rather than how we look when we first turn up.'

The chairman of the panel nodded acknowledgement that John had finished. 'Thank-you for that Mr Coyle and thank-you for attending today. We will be in touch.' He gestured with his outstretched arm towards the door.

John shook the hands of the panel members, thanked them and left with a bad feeling that he had been ruled out even before he opened his mouth based on the assumption, by the interview panel, that he was a money-grabbing greedy property developer looking for kicks in the aftermath of catastrophic natural disasters.

10 ... **Grandad gives us money**

Moments after the crash, Wednesday, April 11, 1984: 'What are YOU doing here?' Five-year-old Sally Whisper was surprised to see her school headmaster. And even more surprised that all the noise had stopped. More than that. Nobody moved. At all.

'Come sit with me Sally.' The headmaster patted the seat next to his own on a soft inviting sofa. 'I need to ask you a couple of things.'

Sally let go of her older brother's hand, gave her younger brother a kiss on the cheek and settled on the sofa. She looked up at the headmaster. 'What do you want to know?' She always liked to be helpful.

He handed her a tissue for her tears. 'You'll be out of here in no time. Help is on its way.'

Sally wiped her eyes. 'Am I in trouble?'

'No. No. Not at all.' The headmaster rested his hand on her head for reassurance. 'But I am.'

'What sort of trouble sir?'

He looked around at the mayhem and stunned faces. 'Well Sally. This bus is a mess.'

The little girl nodded and looked at the debris and injured passengers.

'I'm going to need help clearing up. Some of the passengers will need to stay with me.'

'I can help,' offered Sally with a toothy grin.

The headmaster returned her smile. 'You're very kind, but you'll be needed at home.'

Sally laughed. 'Mum and Dad do everything at home.'

'That's why I need to talk to you Sally. Your mum and dad may need to help clear up the mess. I need 16 helpers.'

Sally pictured herself at home doing the cooking and cleaning. 'I could probably look after my little brother. I do most of the time anyway. He's a good boy.'

'He's a lucky lad. I'm sure you'll do a good job.'

'Grandma and Grandad could help you. They're sat with Mum and Dad. They have lots of spare time. They haven't got jobs. They play Scrabble all day and walk the dog.'

'Yes. Maybe. I'll need either your parents or your grandparents. Who would you prefer me to take?'

Sally looked down at her shoes while scratching her head above her ear, deep in thought. 'How long do you need them for?'

'A very long time.' The headmaster raised his eyebrows. 'Very long.'

Sally scratched harder. She didn't want to choose. 'Will they just have to tidy the bus then come home?'

'When they have finished here, they need to come with me to heaven. There's lots of paperwork to sort. They'll miss your birthday and Christmas too.'

Sally screwed up her face and tears welled up in her big brown eyes. The headmaster gave her a hug and comforted her for a while. After sobbing for a couple of minutes, she looked up again. 'Grandma told me about heaven and hell.'

The headmaster was intrigued. 'What did she tell you?'

'Hell is horrible.'

'Any more?'

'I haven't finished yet.'

'Sorry.'

'It's a big room with seats all around the outside full of skinny, starving people. In the middle of the room is a huge table packed with lovely food of all kinds. Pink wafer biscuits, party rings, chocolate fingers and sausage rolls.'

'But the people are starving?'

'Yes. Because there is an electric fence three feet from the table, all the way round, and they all have six-foot chop-sticks tied to their arms. So they can reach the food over the fence but can't get it in their mouths.'

'Ooh. Sounds awful. So much food and nothing to eat. What about heaven?'

'That's the funny thing,' smiled Sally. 'It's just the same, but the people are all happy, smiling and well fed.'

'No chopsticks or electric fence?'

'Yes chopsticks. Like I said. Just the same. One big room, table full of food, electric fence and six-foot chopsticks tied to their arms.'

'But they're all well fed?'

'Yes,' beamed Sally. 'Because they are nice people in heaven. They all feed each other.'

'Aah. That's nice. I think I will get on well with your grandma.'

Sally frowned. 'I haven't chosen yet. I never said Grandma.'

'Fair enough. What do you think then?'

'Well. I love them all, but Mum and Dad are always so busy and they tell us off a lot. Grandad gives us money and Grandma has lots of stories.'

Sally looked round at her brothers. 'Can I ask Mark and Tom?'

The headmaster shook his head. 'Sorry. It's your choice. Try and think of the good times you've had.'

Sally scratched her head again. 'Dad makes us fight for our pocket money.'

'And that's good?'

'Oh yes.' Sally sensed the headmaster's doubt. 'He puts the pocket money at one end of the front room. We take it in turns to try and run past him and pick it up. He's on his hands and knees and fights us off.' She pointed at the headmaster as if she were correcting him. 'He doesn't hurt us.'

'That's good.'

'Then he lets us cut his hair.'

The headmaster had fresh doubts.

Sally put him straight again. 'We don't ACTUALLY cut it. We have Lego and drumsticks. We run them through his hair and pretend we're at the barbers.'

'Do you do a good job?'

'Oh yes. Very good.'

'What about your mum?'

'She can be annoying. I have some lovely red wellies and she won't let me wear them for school. It's not fair. They're my favourites, but she always looks after us when we're poorly and she makes delicious sticky biscuits with oats.'

'Sounds nice.'

'And belly of pork. She does that for tea sometimes. And blancmange. That's lovely. Tapioca. Mmmm.'

'What about your grandparents?'

'They never tell us off.'

'Why not?'

'Don't know. They're just really nice. I can even wear my red wellies in their house.'

'Do you fight your grandad for money?'

'No. He finds it in our hair.'

The headmaster looked confused.

'After we've been for a visit, he reaches over to our hair and says "ooh, what's this?" Then he opens his hand and there's a 50p coin. We have to share it but it doesn't split three ways. That's a bit annoying. But he's funny when we eat at their house. Before Grandma brings out the pudding, which is always something really special, he rubs his hands together, opens his eyes wide and sucks in through his lips like he's drinking through a straw. Makes a whistling sound. We always laugh at him.'

'Sounds nice.'

'And Grandma's food is lovely. She always has sweets for us as well. And clothes. Gets them from jumble sales. There's always something good. And she tells stories.'

'Tough choice then.'

Sally scratched her head again.

'Who's it going to be Sally?' The headmaster pushed her for an answer.

Sally thought about all the serious talks her parents had about how to pay for everything. Grandad gives us money. She looked at her brothers as she gave her answer. 'My parents will help you.' Turning back, the headmaster had gone. There was an old man stood where the sofa had been. 'You keep still kids. Stay well away from that door okay?'

Sally looked back at the open side door of the bus. She snuggled up against her older brother who reached a protective arm around her.

11 ... **Coffee break**

Day of the crash, Wednesday, April 11, 1984: Opposite the crash site was a passing place cut into the hillside with four round plastic white tables in a row. Each had four plastic moulded white chairs and a coloured umbrella with matching cushions on the seats. Sat at the table furthest from the wreck of the bus were four young men. They had a light blue umbrella.

'Denise will be well pissed off,' said Twig with the same serious tone he normally used when breaking very bad news, like unfavourable football results. 'She was looking forward to the wedding.' Marco, Rozzer and Dean all nodded with equally serious faces. 'Don't suppose she'll miss YOU much Marco, but missing out on that party…' Twig sighed. 'She'll be gutted.'

Rozzer looked across at the plume of smoke rising gently from the upturned bus. 'Helen'll miss me. She'll struggle with no money and a baby on the way.

Dean leant forward with his face resting in his hands.

'Hey Deano.' Marco felt a bit responsible. They had only been on the bus because of his stag week. 'At least we're all still together.'

Dean tilted his head back a little and his eyes appeared above his hands.

'Come on mate. So we're dead. It's not the end of the world.' Marco's big smile immediately fell away as he thought about what he had just said. Maybe it was the end of the world. What happened next? Why were they all sat at a table opposite the crashed bus?

Dean looked deep into Marco's eyes and held his gaze for a few seconds. 'I'm frightened Marco.'

Twig looked at each of his friends in turn. 'So am I. Maybe it is the end of the world. What happens now?'

A smile spread across Marco's face as he looked past Twig. An attractive Greek girl, mid twenties, was walking towards them with a tray of beers. 'That's what happens next.' Marco rubbed his hands together as the girl handed out the beers. 'Cheers Zorbette. You're a star.'

The girl stopped and faced Marco with a blank expression.

He looked up at her wondering what he had done wrong.

'My name is Keres … not Zorbette … Keres. Say it Marco.'

'Sorry Keres.' Marco was suddenly a little nervous. How did she know his name? And worse than that, he had a bad feeling about the name Keres, but he wasn't sure why.

Dean tilted his head forward again and his hands once again covered his eyes. He knew why they recognised the name Keres. She was the barman's sister who had drowned three rowdy guests in a bucket of beer.

Keres walked back down the road with her empty tray and round the next bend.

A middle-aged couple sat down at the next table. It had a pale yellow umbrella with matching seat covers. A young man with his back to the four boys took their order before walking past the boys towards the bend in the road.

'Thanatos,' shouted Dean. 'You alright?'

The barman stopped. 'No Dean. I'm Hypnos. I'm good thanks. Nice to see you all again.'

Dean felt the same uneasiness that Marco had felt. Who were these people and how did they know the boys' names?

Marco beckoned Hypnos over with an upward nod of his head. 'Is your bother here as well?'

'He is, but he's busy on the bus at the moment.'

The boys all looked at each other.

Dean had a lot of questions. 'Is he spoofing other passengers to see who dies?'

'Not exactly, but something like that.'

'So our spoof game was for real then?'

'Oh yes,' replied Hypnos quickly, almost as if it were a stupid question.

'So if you can decide whether we live or die …' Dean paused. 'Who are you?'

'I am the God of Sleep. I don't deal with death.'

'But Thanatos?' asked Dean, who was starting to piece things together.

'He's my twin, the God of Death.'

Hypnos started to walk away as the boys all sat open-mouthed struggling to get their heads round what was happening.

Dean shouted after Hypnos. 'Please. One more thing.'

Hypnos stopped again.

'What about Keres?'

'She's the God of Violent Death.' With that Hypnos turned and walked beyond the bend in the road.

When the boys finally stopped staring blankly down the road, they turned back towards the bus and saw Thanatos walking towards the tables carrying a shoe box. He stopped at the far table with a peach coloured umbrella and placed the shoe box on one of the chairs before turning back towards the bus.

'Thanatos,' shouted Twig.

He turned and walked up to the boys' table. 'Twig. You okay?'

'You should have told us what we were spoofing for.'

Thanatos smiled warmly. 'I did.'

'But we thought you were joking.'

'I know.'

Twig had no comeback for that.

Dean was still looking for answers.

'Can you tell us why your sister is here? Was somebody murdered or was the crash caused intentionally?'

'No harm in telling you I suppose. The crash was an accident. The road was slippery from a burst of rain, the driver's reactions were slightly dulled by a couple of beers and his concentration was broken by some unexpected news. No murders. Just an accident. Keres takes care of violent death, but as Rozzer's life ended so horrifically, she helped with that.'

Rozzer hadn't been listening closely as he was dwelling on how Helen would cope with their baby when it was born, but he immediately perked up when he heard his name. 'How did I die then?'

'Well … you won't like this.'

Rozzer opened his eyes wider.

'The back window was smashed and gone after the first roll. Dean and Marco were thrown onto the ceiling first and on the second roll, Twig landed on them before you Rozzer. You hit them and your arm went out of the window, before being trapped between the road and the sliding bus.'

The boys winced.

'You were pulled under the bus just before it ploughed through the crash barrier.'

'So where's my body now?' Rozzer screwed up his face.

'What's left of it is where the crash barrier used to be. The bus is now pivoting on your body and a lot of people's lives are hanging in the balance.'

Rozzer felt sick. He wretched but nothing came up.

'Is the bus going to fall?' Dean was curious.

'Probably not, but it could,' replied Thanatos after a brief pause for thought.

'Busy day for you if it does.'

'Too busy. If the bus falls, I might overshoot my target.'

'You knew it was going to crash back at the hotel, so why don't you know whether it will fall.' Dean was filling in the blanks.

'Well actually. I knew it would PROBABLY crash. And I know it PROBABLY won't fall, but nothing is ever definite. It's only the introduction of chance that creates reality.'

Dean had to think about that one, but he still had other questions. 'Why are we drinking beer watching the bus and where will we go next?'

'Nothing happens until I fill these four tables and where you go next depends on what you believe and what you don't believe. It's down to you and whatever religion has dominated your life.'

'What if I'm not religious?' Dean had never been to church for anything other than weddings and funerals.

'You'll probably be recycled.'

Dean raised his eyebrows. 'What? Re-incarnation?'

Thanatos held out his arms. 'Again Dean. It depends what you do and don't believe.'

'I'm Roman Catholic. Where will I go?' asked Marco.

'Do you believe in heaven and hell?' Thanatos doubted that Marco were a devout Catholic.

'S'pose so,' said Marco with very little conviction.

'I expect you'll be recycled. You need commitment to get to heaven.'

Dean had another question. 'So if you are a really bad person, but don't believe in hell, you're safe? You go for recycling?'

'Not that straightforward.'

'What then?'

'You may still wind up in hell, because your actions have been collectively considered evil by all religions that you may or may not have turned your back on. So the universally bad apples are still rejected.'

Hypnos served drinks to the middle-aged couple at the yellow table while Keres placed a tray on the table with the peach umbrella and cushions.

'Coffee,' Keres shouted to her brothers. Hypnos joined her.

'Excuse me. Time for a coffee break.'

'Just one thing,' Dean asked.

Thanatos looked at Dean. 'Go on.'

'What are these places like? I can guess at heaven and hell, but what's recycling?'

'Simple answer. I don't know. I'm like your bus driver. I just deliver you to the airport.' With that he headed for the peach table and sipped his coffee.

'Can't stand that Rozzer bloke,' said Keres.

'Well Keres. You've made a nasty mess of his body.'

'Could have done worse. It was too quick. No pain. No fear.' Keres had venom in her voice. 'Anyway, I'm glad you chose him Thana.'

'But I didn't.'

'Course you did. You had a fair idea who would win the spoof game.'

'Well yes. A fair idea. But I didn't know.'

'You're such a bloody jobsworth Thana. There's plenty of nasty buggers I would happily cull given half the chance.'

'But it has to be a bit random. Death can't be means tested. If it's not random, the world would be full of thoroughly nice people and the equilibrium of life would be completely thrown off balance. Wouldn't work. That's the rule and I'm sticking with it.'

Keres sipped her coffee and stared at the smoking bus for a while. 'What caused the smoke Thana?'

'Oil spilled from the cracked engine on the hot metal.'

'Is there goin' to be a fire?'

'Probably not.'

101

'Explosion?'

'Don't think so. Most of the petrol is at the back so even if a fire starts near the engine ...' Thanatos paused mid sentence and looked across at the angle of the bus. Now he thought aloud, 'Mind you, if the bus tilts further, the spilled oil may trickle towards the petrol tank at the back.'

'So it could blow up?'

'S'pose so!'

'And fall off the cliff?'

'Could. Yes.'

They both looked at each other with raised eyebrows.

'Don't think it will though.' Thanatos didn't sound convincing. His work with the dying passengers would have been wasted if he ended up taking the lot.

Keres took a sip of coffee. 'What's in the shoe box Thana?'

Thanatos frowned apologetically. 'Nothing yet. It's for the courier's unborn baby.'

Keres was outraged and stood up pointing a finger at Thanatos.

The middle-aged couple and the four boys all looked round.

'What's the matter with you Thana? An unborn child has the purest soul of us all. It hasn't had chance to commit sin yet. What random situation did you contrive to use an unborn child as part of your quota?'

Thanatos was a little surprised by her strength of feeling. He would have been quite within his rights to learn nothing about all 49 people on the bus and pick his 16 entirely at random, which could have included the unborn baby. But no. He had gone to the trouble of getting to know them so that he could make an informed choice. Not total means testing, but it was to some extent. He had to maintain a random element to abide by the rules and he had given the unborn baby a fighting chance. He had actually expected the baby to live. His intention had been for the courier to kill off the driver.

'I didn't intend for the baby to die.'

'Not good enough Thanatos. I expect better from you.'

Thanatos felt he was being unfairly castigated and snapped back. 'Strictly speaking Keres, I bent the rules to give the baby a good chance of living. So I misjudged one person. Aren't I allowed the odd mistake now and then?'

'So you agree it was a mistake.' Keres felt she was making progress.

'Yes.'

'Why don't you do something about it then?'

'I can't. You know I can't. The job's done. The choice was made.'

'Yes you can. You can change your mind.'

'I can't. It's done. Before the day began, we all knew what was going to happen and we're here to finish the job.'

'No Thanatos. You knew what was PROBABLY going to happen. Things could turn out differently. There's a chance that you could change what choices have been made. You know how it works. It's only the introduction of chance that creates reality.'

12 ... **Jane and Mabel**

Almost a year before the crash, Saturday, July 23, 1983: Rip It Up by Orange Juice was playing in the Horizon Bar of the Dover to Calais cross channel ferry. Sisters Jane and Mabel Chimera had been at each other's throats for more than fifty years and sat on high stools arguing over who should pay for their drinks.

'Which part of "I got the first one" is confusing you?' asked Jane, who was almost two years older than her sister.

'You can be such a bitch and it comes so naturally. I got the last two in a row last night.'

'You're insane. How can you count that? It was happy hour … two for the price of one.'

Mabel was livid. Every previous happy hour had been treated as non-happy hour. Jane was moving the goalposts. 'I can't believe you Jane.' Mabel ushered away the barman with a flick of the wrist. He was anxious to move on to other customers. 'No. I take that back. I can believe you. It's so typical of you. You've been looking down your nose at me as if I'm hired help since the day I was born.'

'Bollocks Mabel,' Jane thundered, before a slight hint of embarrassment. She briefly looked around at the sour faces surrounding her. It was enough to prompt a temporary climb-down. She reached in her purse, pulled out a fiver and thrust it towards the barman. 'Don't expect a tip young man. Gin and tonic without a slice of lemon. Unbelievable.'

The girls' parents came from a poor background but had worked hard and prospered. They had doted on their two girls. Jane and Mabel were given everything their parents had missed out on as children. The girls had wanted for nothing, but as the years passed, the girls' demands grew beyond their parents' means.

A point came where the anger of missing out was greater than the joy of getting what they wanted. The girls were thoroughly spoilt to the extent that neither of them ever found a man prepared to tolerate them in a relationship long enough to marry. Jane had been engaged and got as far as her wedding day, but an on-going row over the honeymoon ended with the would-be husband walking out of the church just before making his vows.

Jane had demanded that he sell his vintage Alvis to pay for a two-week cruise to Hawaii. The Alvis owner married someone else two years later and took the old car on his honeymoon to the Lake District.

The girls' me-me-me attitude resulted in an intense lifelong sibling rivalry, the like of which hadn't been seen since Cane murdered Abel 3,000 years ago. It would be fair to say the girls deserved each other.

'This isn't over Mabel. You have just humiliated me.'

Mabel almost choked on her gin. 'You have to be joking. It was your turn. Okay you looked bad. So what! The whole world doesn't revolve around you.'

'Says you.' Disbelief. 'Who defaced the family album?'

Mabel slammed her glass down on the bar. 'Give it a rest Jane. You beat me with that stick every time we have an argument.'

'And rightly so. I am the favoured daughter and you have spent your whole life consumed with jealousy.'

'Right. Let's clear this up once and for all. I was six years old and you take things on face value at that age. I was wrong. Our parents didn't favour you. There just happened to be more pictures of you as a baby in the album because you were born first. By the time I came along they had two babies and no time for photos.'

'So spiteful Mabel pulled out all the photos of me and put them on the fire. Six or not, that's pretty vicious.'

'Unkind yes, but who isn't at six? As I saw it, we had no family album. We had a Mum, Dad and Jane album. Any kid would feel bad.'

'You're wrong. But on reflection, I don't blame you. I WAS the favourite. Understandable. I'm brighter, better looking, funnier.'

'Rubbish. Truth is, they spoiled us both. I was just as much a favourite as you were.'

Jane smiled smugly. 'So why did they think about aborting you then?'

Mabel's face tensed. 'You take that back now. That's just nasty. Plain nasty.'

'But true.' Jane slowly nodded with both eyebrows raised, or rather, painted lines where her eyebrows had once been.

'Any lie that suits. You'll throw anything in to get one over on me, but that just isn't true.'

'It is. I overheard them about ten years ago just before Dad died.'

'There's no reason why they would have even considered abortion.'

'You were an accident. Unwanted. They had planned a five-year gap and wanted a boy. They didn't want you. That's probably why they hardly took any photos of their "mistake".'

'Well, there's no way you were the favourite. Dad once told me you were the jealous one when I was a baby. You used to hit me in my pram when you thought nobody was looking. But you were seen. Dad thought you were trying to get me in trouble. Making me cry so I wound them up. Didn't work. They saw you.'

'Get stuffed mistake.'

'Bugger off baby basher.'

'Abort me. Abort me. I'm a spoilt bitch,' mocked Jane.

It was too much. Mabel threw what was left of her gin and tonic in her sister's face. 'I was NOT a mistake.'

Jane had finished her drink, but threw the remains of two ice cubes in Mabel's face. 'Bitch. You were. Ask Mum.'

They both stopped and it went quiet. They put their empty glasses on the bar and faced each other with confused faces.

'Where is Mum?' asked Mabel.

The sisters had driven to Dover from Richmond that morning. They were treating their mother to a French day trip.

'Last time I saw her was when we parked in the long-stay car park at Dover.' Jane rubbed her chin. She was deep in thought. 'You did go back for her after we picked up our tickets didn't you?'

'I thought you did.'

'Shit,' they both said, almost in unison.

They looked at each other in disbelief. 'She's still in the car park at Dover.' Mabel put her hand to her forehead.

'She'll make my life hell on the way home,' Jane reached for the payphone at the end of the bar. 'We'd better call the police.'

'If she forgets her medication. Ooh. Well I don't know what would happen. I hope she's not eating in my car. Greasy fingers. Yuck.' Mabel screwed up her face.

'Hello. Is that the police?' asked Jane.

'No.'

'I need the police quick.'

'No you don't.'

'Yes I do thank-you very much.' Jane was indignant.

'The only person you need is me,' said a soft assured voice on the other end of the line.'

Jane held the handset out in front of her and looked at it with disgust. 'Nutter,' she exclaimed, before putting the handset back up to her ear.

'And who are you?'

The barman took the phone out of Jane's hand and hung it up. 'He is the Grim Reaper.'

Jane looked totally confused.

'He … no … I … I am the Grim Reaper.' The barman looked into Jane's eyes, before gesturing with his arm for her to look around the rest of the bar.

She turned. Around her was the inside of a wrecked bus. It was silent. There was smoke but it didn't move. There were bodies, some alive, some dead, but none of them moved.

Some people were open-mouthed as if they had stopped mid-sentence. There was a strong smell. She didn't recognise it. There were three children huddled together by the open side door of the bus, but through the open door, she could see no road, just empty space. Looking towards the smashed back window, she saw sky and hill tops. Towards the front, there was the road. They were balanced on the edge of a cliff.

Mabel breathed in sharply and squealed. She grabbed Jane's arm. She was looking at a pile of debris near the window. 'Jane. That's you and me down there.'

Jane looked back at the barman. 'What's going on?'

'These are on the house.' He put two glasses on the bar. 'Like I said, I'm the Grim Reaper. You've been in a crash.'

'Two minutes ago, we were on a cross channel ferry.'

'Two minutes ago, you faced death. Your life flashed before your eyes in a fraction of a second. Not your whole life. Just the key moments. Things that had a real and lasting impact. Good or bad. Mostly bad in your case.'

Jane and Mabel both looked at their motionless blood-stained bodies.

'So we're dead?' asked Jane.

'Almost.' Grim nodded.

'And you're giving us one final drink before you whisk us off to heaven?'

Grim smiled. 'Something like that.'

'Make it a double then.' Jane pushed her drink back across the bar.

Grim ignored it. 'I'm giving you both one last chance. I don't have to. After all, you are probably the two most selfish people I have ever come across.'

Despite the insult, their faces lit up.

'We will survive then?' asked Mabel hopefully.

Grim recoiled. 'Can't say. Nothing's ever that easy.'

The women looked at each other. Not pleased. They were used to always getting their own way.

'One last chance to survive.'

The sisters waited.

'You are both extremely selfish, but the fact that you found yourselves back on the ferry on the day you forgot your mother and left her in the car park, suggests to me that, in a small way, you recognise you are selfish. That counts for something. Not much. But something.'

Grim came round the front of the bar and sat at one of the tall stools next to the women.

'Can either of you tell me something you have done in your lives when you put somebody else first, a genuine act of kindness?'

Jane rubbed her chin.

Mabel put her hand to her forehead.

Thirty seconds later, Jane jumped. 'I know.'

'Okay. Go on,' urged Grim.

'When we were kids. Mabel was about four. She got a pan stuck on her head. One of those with curved sides so the inside is wider than the opening. She forced her head in and couldn't get it out. We had to call the fire brigade to cut it off.'

'Yes. I remember.' Not one of Mabel's fondest memories.

'Mabel was in floods of tears. I held her hand while the firemen cut through the pan. Mum and Dad said I was a big help. Couldn't have done it without me.'

The barman looked deep into Jane's eyes.

'How's that?' she asked proudly.

'No good.'

'Why not?'

'Wrong motivation.'

'What do you mean?'

'Looks to me like your sister, with a pan firmly stuck on her head, got all the attention and you didn't like it. I think you held her hand to make sure you were involved. Share the moment. Still selfish. Nope. No good.'

Jane pointed angrily at Grim, but as she opened her mouth to protest, he stopped her.

'Accept it.' He reached slowly forward and gently pushed her hand back down. 'Question me and you weaken your case. I know more than you think.'

'My turn.'

'Go on Mabel.'

'Couple of years after the pan thing, we were both in the school play. Mum and Dad came to watch and both fell asleep.'

'Yes,' nodded Jane, still angry forty-something years later.

'Jane was one of the main characters and almost refused to complete the final scene. Her face was red from crying and she didn't want everyone knowing why. There would be questions. Anyway, I gave her a hug, reassured her and persuaded her to finish the show.'

'Right.' Grim nodded but didn't look convinced.

'I comforted her,' Mabel shouted. Why wasn't he giving her due credit?

'Yes Mabel. You hugged her, but you were probably comforting yourself more than Jane. You were just as upset by your parents sleeping through the show.'

Mabel grimaced. 'There's no pleasing you. What do we have to do?'

'Well, it's good that you are finally using the word "we" instead of "I", but it's all a bit too late.'

'Come on Grim,' Jane pleaded. 'One last chance you said.'

Grim poured himself a drink, took a sip and placed the glass down on the bar. 'Tell you what. I'll try something.'

'Yey,' they squealed together.

'Mabel.'

'Yup.'

'See those three kids over there by the open door.'

Mabel looked round. 'Yeah.'

'I'll give you a choice.'

Mabel nodded.

'At the moment Mabel, you are dying. Within a minute you will be dead, but you may choose one of those three kids to take your place. Pick a child and they will die instead of you, or accept your own death.'

Outwardly Mabel was appalled. Inwardly she was jumping cartwheels and popping Champagne.

'That's a cruel thing you are making me do. The hardest choice I have ever had to make.' She looked from one child to the next. There was a boy of about two, a girl of about five and a second boy a bit older again. Mabel had already picked out the older boy. He had dirty knees, but she waited a little longer so Grim was convinced that the choice was hard for her. Eventually she whined and looked at Grim with an agonised expression.

'I don't know. They're such cute kids.'

'I need your choice,' urged Grim.

'Okay. Okay. The older boy.' Mabel held her hands up to cover her face. She didn't want her expression giving away her relief.

'Mabel.' Grim pulled her hands away from her face and looked into her eyes. 'You have failed the test. If you had shown me a selfless act of kindness, I would have spared you.'

Mabel's eyes opened wide with horror, but before she could react, she found herself stood outside the bus.

Back in the bus Grim turned to Jane. 'Your turn. You or one of the children?'

Jane turned away from Grim and looked in the direction of the three kids. She wasn't looking at the three kids. She just wanted to hide her face from Grim while she tried to second guess him. If she chose a child, Jane would share her sister's fate, but if she chose herself to die, he would know she had learned from Mabel's failed test. She must be missing something, but the only certain outcome seemed to be following Mabel. She had to take a chance.

'Take me. Save the children.'

'Okay,' said Grim.

Jane found herself outside the bus stood next to Mabel. She saw Grim drinking coffee with a couple of friends in a cluster of white tables with coloured umbrellas. She marched over.

'Why did you take me?'

The barman sipped his coffee before looking up. 'That was your choice.'

'Mabel chose the kid and died. I had to choose myself.'

'Ask yourself why you chose yourself?'

Jane thought but didn't answer.

'You saw your sister take the test. I was looking for a selfless act of kindness. You didn't do that. You made the only choice you thought would save your neck. The welfare of the kids never crossed your mind.'

'You don't know that. You don't know why I made that choice. You can't read my mind.'

The barman took another sip of coffee before looking up again at Jane. 'Oh, but I can. Not your deepest thoughts, but I can read your conscious thoughts and that's why I set the test.'

Jane's jaw dropped.

'Yes. You said the right thing, but your thoughts were ugly.' He pointed towards the only remaining empty table. 'Please. Take a seat. There is no option to appeal. Fight me and things could go horribly wrong for you.'

The women did as they were told and headed for the empty table. The morning clouds had cleared and the sun was hot. The lilac umbrella only cast shade on one of the four chairs. Jane and Mabel both placed one hand on the back of the shaded chair at the same time. An argument followed.

As the barman finished his coffee, Keres challenged him. 'Were they the same kids whose parents are two tables down from here?'

'That's right.'

'How can you do that? I thought you had saved those kids when you took their parents.'

'I did.'

'Sounds to me like you just offered those odious women the chance to live in exchange for one of the kids.'

'Yes I did, but it was never going to happen. Those two women were dead as soon as they got on the bus. I didn't need to talk to them at all. I just felt like it.'

'But you said there has to be a random element in the choice of everyone who dies.'

'There was.'

'What then?'

'I chose five specific seats before the bus picked up anybody. Those two women took two of them. Totally by chance.'

Keres slowly raised her head in realisation, but turned round sharply as Jane started shouting at Mabel.

'Which part of "I got here first" don't you understand?'

The barman looked up at the clear blue sky just as a single cloud moved slowly over the sun.

13 ... **I need an answer**

Nearly 31 years before the crash, August 29, 1952: Gordon and Mary Teal held hands as the number 63 bus pulled out of Southside Hospital and headed past the derelict munitions factory on its way towards town centre. The factory had been closed since just after the war and high fences had been built around the site for the protection of the public, although there were one or two places where kids with more curiosity than sense had squeezed through to get a closer look.

Mary smiled warmly at her husband. 'That's where we met. Horrible place. Hardest work I've ever done. Searched on your way in, but can't help loving the old place. If I hadn't worked there, we'd never have met.'

Gordon kissed Mary's cheek and squeezed her hand a little tighter before wincing and reaching for his hip.

'You okay Honey?'

'Yeah. Think so. Must have moved too fast.'

Mary watched the munitions factory as it disappeared behind them. 'I remember every word you said when we met. Like it was yesterday.'

Gordon closed his eyes and was back in the cloakroom of the factory after a long shift, looking for his bike saddle, which he presumed his friends had removed as a prank.

'Lost something?' Mary Pimlico asked.

Gordon was flustered. He had noticed this pretty young lady in the factory a few times. She had a sweet smile and a nice pair of legs. He had been hoping to meet her. He was nervous and lost for words. Internally he shook himself and concentrated. 'Yes. Yes I have.' He said. Nothing more.

Mary waited before asking, 'What? What have you lost?'

Again she smiled warmly and Gordon had to focus his mind. He must be staring. 'My. My err…'

'Your bike saddle?' asked Mary.

'Yes,' Gordon replied quickly and with great surprise. 'How did you know?'

'Wild guess,' said Mary handing Gordon his bike saddle.

Gordon's eyes danced around the room. 'Where was it?'

'On the hook under my coat.' She held her hands up. 'Nothing to do with me,' she exclaimed.

'Oh I know. Never thought for a second. It's my friends. Such wags.'

They headed for the bike sheds and Gordon pushed his seat back on the shaft.

'It's loose, but should be okay.'

Mary grabbed her bike. 'Which way are you heading?'

'Up near the police station on Talk Drive.'

'I'm not far from there. I'll ride with you.'

'Great.' Gordon reached his hand out across their two bikes. 'Gordon Teal.'

'Mary.' She shook his hand gently. 'Mary Pimlico.'

'Pleased to meet you Mary Pimlico.'

The brakes screeched as the bus came to a halt. Mary helped Gordon out of his seat and down the steps.

'Thanks very much.'

The driver nodded.

Mary supported Gordon as they made slow progress towards Granville Terrace and home.

'You sit down while I make a cup of tea Honey.' Mary led Gordon towards the floral sofa.

Gordon resisted. 'I think I'd prefer my dentist chair Babe.'

Mary looked away in disgust. 'When we move, that's going to the tip. No arguments. I'm having a new three piece.'

'Yes. Yes.' Gordon agreed for the sake of peace and quiet.

He leaned back and adjusted the seat until he was almost lying down.

Five minutes later Mary returned with his tea, pumped the chair back up straight and handed him his drink.

'Sit properly or you'll get indigestion.'

'Aww. My hip felt better when I was out flat.'

'If you want to lie down, go to bed.' Mary liked things done properly.

Before sitting down with her tea, she flicked on the radio. It took the valves a moment to warm up and the reception wasn't good. It never was on an evening, and sometimes wandered out of tune, but she was anxious to hear the news.

Gordon and Mary should have been in Lynmouth, Devon, two weeks earlier. It would have been their first holiday after nine years together, five of them as a married couple. The plan had been to ride their bikes the 150 miles to Lynmouth, where they had booked a B&B for four nights, but a pain in Gordon's hip had forced them to cancel.

Gordon had considered himself extremely unlucky when x-rays revealed a German bullet lodged in his hip, which he had been carrying around since the Normandy landings without knowing. It hadn't hurt for years and he never even knew he had been shot.

He remembered a thump in his hip soon after landing on the beach, but it didn't knock him over. He later had a plaster slapped on it and was sent back out.

The doctors had decided to remove the bullet as soon as possible after seeing the x-rays and the Lynmouth trip had been cancelled. In the days that followed, Gordon's opinion changed. He now considered himself very lucky.

Mary adjusted the dial to get a better signal and checked her watch. News was on the hour every hour. 'Can't believe what's happened, 34 people killed, 420 homeless.'

Freak floods had devastated the seaside resort of Lynmouth.

'A hundred buildings destroyed, including the B&B we booked.'

'We could be dead Gordon. Doesn't bear thinking about.'

'Yeah. And you're fussing over my favourite chair.'

Mary sighed and pumped the lever to lower the back of her husband's seat. She put down her cup and gave him a hug. 'I love you Gordon Teal.'

'I love you too Mary.' Gordon kissed her forehead. 'And I love the German sniper who accidentally saved our lives.'

There was a burst of interference before a quiet moment. Then the time signal started. 'Pip, pip, pip ... and silence.'

They both looked at each other before turning to the radio.

Mary turned back to Gordon. 'Only three pips?' She took a closer look at the radio. Seemed okay. There was a soft orange glow showing the needle over the frequency chart. There was a gentle hum.

'It's definitely on.'

'Please Mary. Take a seat.' Mary almost jumped out of her skin. The radio had spoken to her. She sat down briefly before getting back up to join her husband.

The radio presenter continued. 'I need an answer.'

The presenter was talking to them. Mary held Gordon's hand tight.

'Look out of the front window,' continued the radio presenter.

It was a late summer evening, but still light outside. Mary pulled back the net curtain and gasped as she looked down the cliff to the jagged rocks below. There were gentle waves lapping against the shoreline. Mary lost her footing as the house tilted a little more over the edge of the cliff before rocking gently back.

'Time is running out. If you don't make a choice I will have to take you both.'

A tear rolled down Mary's cheek. She looked into Gordon's eyes as she remembered where they were. 'Let me go Gordon. My injuries are worse than yours.'

'Never like to complicate things,' continued the radio. 'But Gordon's blood clot is moving steadily towards his lungs. It's going to hurt and could be a problem.'

'What about Mary?' asked Gordon.

'Not good, but no worse than when I first spoke to you. You have stopped the bleeding. That's the main thing.'

'So if I go with you,' Gordon was trying to strengthen his case. 'Mary will make a full recovery?'

The Grim Reaper didn't want to give too much away. 'I've probably told you too much already. You're both in a bad way. You're both about the same age and you both have roughly the same life expectancy should you survive today. But I have to take one of you. Like I said, this is the third time you have each been on my list.'

'What were the other times?' Mary asked.

There was another surge of interference. Mary tapped the top of the radio and it cleared.

'The crashed car in your garden, I already told you about. You were both on my list for Lynmouth and I had Gordon down for the Normandy landings.'

'And Mary's other time?' asked Gordon.

There was more interference before the sound cleared.

'Pip, pip, pip, peeep.'

14 ... **Russian roulette**

Eighteen years before the crash, Friday, January 8, 1965: 'This has got nothing to do with the Green Street robbery. I shagged your mother a few times and it pissed you off.' Juan Gonzalez was roped with his back against a metal support pillar in the main filling room of the derelict Southside munitions factory.

The building had been empty for 20 years and was due for redevelopment as a university. The whole site had been fenced off to avoid any health risk from contamination. There was a strong smell of sulphur and dampness. Vegetation filled the crumbling building despite the limited light. The windows had been boarded up, but skylights filled the factory with a yellow wintry glow.

Pedro Raphael, a man of very few words in his mid twenties, had never had a conventional job. He always took what he wanted and the town of Southside, near London, was his home. Burglary had been his life since early childhood. When Pedro was four years old, Swifty, one of his mother's partners, none of them lasted long, pushed Pedro through a tiny window above the cloakroom of a large house near the hospital. Pedro opened the front door.

There was a lot of cash in the house. Swifty took it and ran. Pedro had to walk two miles home and neither he nor his mother Leah, saw Swifty again.

Leah struggled to provide for Pedro and his three younger brothers, but by the age of ten, Pedro was the main earner. Pedro never had any moral issues with taking what he needed. The only thing of value to him was his family. Beyond that he cared about where he lived, but only as a resource. He vigorously guarded his immediate neighbourhood from rival criminals.

Juan Gonzalez, also mid twenties, had stepped over the line. He was from the other side of town but had met Leah at the railway station. She had been cleaning the toilets when he had been meeting a business associate. He took her out for a drink the next day but there were no more dates after that. He called every now and then, when it suited him, never when it suited Leah.

'Fuck you Juan. This is my side of town.'

'One job and you bundle me away to this shit-hole.'

'Shut the fuck up. If I let this go, the rest of your scum will follow.' Pedro pulled out a blade, an old army knife he had taken from a large house near Southside Common. 'I'm gonna have to hurt you.'

Juan struggled but the ropes tightened. He was no stranger to violence, but he was alone with Pedro, no witnesses and nobody to question Pedro's actions. There was an unpredictable coldness about this pock-marked young man that un-nerved Juan. He had been warned by one of his business friends not to venture to the western edge of town. 'Pedro Raphael.' The man had shook his head with eyes wide open. 'Nasty bastard. Time bomb. Tick, tick.'

Pedro looked down at the ground rolling the handle of the knife between his fingers like a nervous tennis player toying with his racquet.

'Listen Pedro. Let's talk about this.'

'I told you to shut the fuck up.' Pedro shouted with venom. He didn't want to talk. He wanted to deal with his problem decisively and didn't like his concentration broken. He was calculating in his mind what the possible outcomes might be if he were to sink the knife into Juan's chest.

'Look, Pedro. I heard about the Major and his diamonds in a pub. I had the job all worked out and it was only by chance that he happened to be in Green Lane on the day of the job.'

Pedro had heard enough. He didn't like Juan Gonzalez's scratchy voice and all he had been able to see when he shut his eyes for the past three days was Juan climbing off his mother, wiping his knob on the sheets, pulling his pants up and pushing past him to the front door.

He paced up and down through the puddles on the dirty concrete floor. Then he stopped in front of Juan and looked deep into his eyes, but said nothing.

Juan tensed his muscles and pushed against the ropes. The menace of the silence was worse than when Pedro spoke. 'Listen, there was only a small chance the job would be done this side of town. A small chance.'

'Ha, ha, ha, ha.' Pedro laughed like a machine gun. It was a forced laugh. He had made his mind up. He knew what he must do. 'A small chance eh? Ha, ha, ha, ha.'

Pedro grabbed Juan's collar, twisted it and pulled the man's face close to his own. He spoke through clenched teeth. 'Then I will give you a small chance. I will stab you once. Only once. If you survive, stay the fuck away from here.'

Juan raised his eyebrows and spoke fast with panic in his voice. 'No need. Promise. Let me go. You'll never see me again.'

Pedro gripped Juan's collar tighter and pulled him a little closer, before slamming him back against the pillar, raised his arm and sunk the knife into his chest.

Juan winced. There was a look of horror in his eyes. Then he slumped forward, held only by the ropes.

'Fuck it,' Pedro thought to himself. Killing Juan had not been one of the outcomes he had given much thought to, but it did send out the strongest possible signal.

Pedro rested his forehead in his hand and closed his eyes. Juan was still there, climbing off his mother, but when he opened his eyes, he was no longer in the munitions factory, he was sat at a small table in a bar surrounded by noisy drinkers who were shouting bets at each other and handing over large wads of notes.

His clothes were different. He now wore a white dress shirt, open at the collar with a wide red bandana around his head. Stood to his left was a man in his mid thirties. He wore shiny black shoes, a dark suit and an eye patch over his right eye. He had black hair, gelled and brushed back, and a thin black tie. A cigarette hung from his closed mouth.

Sat facing Pedro was an attractive tanned girl in her late twenties. She looked fiercely at Pedro, pinning him to his seat.

Pedro nodded gently upwards. 'Who are you?'

'Keres.'

'What d'you want?'

She looked at him for a moment. The noise of shouted bets had stopped. 'You are about to die.'

'Fuck off,' Pedro shouted with disgust. He stood up and pushed his way through the crowd. As he brushed past the man with the eye patch he lost his footing briefly. Looking down there were the dead bodies of two women in their fifties. Beyond them was a pile of suitcases and more dead bodies. He could go no further. There was an open window but only empty space beyond.

He looked around. He had never been in a bar like this before. It looked like a bus. He pushed his way to the other end but the door was jammed shut. His every movement was followed by the crowd, which kept quiet and watched. He tried the windows, but there was no way out. Eventually he sat back opposite Keres.

'Okay. What the fuck's going on?'

'You are about to die,' she repeated slowly, with absolute authority.

Pedro was getting impatient. He didn't know where he was or what he was doing there. 'What the fuck you on about?'

'You have been in a bus crash and you are bleeding heavily.' She looked beyond Pedro and pointed.

Pedro turned and breathed in sharply as he saw his flaccid body twisted in a corner of the wreckage.

His heart was racing and his breath was short as he turned back to the table in a panic, but Keres was gone. Juan Gonzalez now sat opposite Pedro. He also wore a white shirt and a red bandana. There was a large red blood stain on the shirt. Juan sat with both hands resting on the table.

Pedro's eyes flicked around the bus. The girl was gone. He looked back at Juan and sneered. 'Okay. What the fuck are YOU doin' here?'

'I've come for you. I'm the Grim Reaper.'

'Grim Reaper my arse. You're Juan fuckin' Gonzalez. Thought I'd taken care of you years ago.'

'I AM the Grim Reaper and you ARE bleeding to death.'

'What the fuck do you want Gonzalez?'

'I'm offering you a chance to live.'

'What a fucking saint.'

The bar was quiet. The watching gamblers' eyes moved in unison from one man to the other.

Juan leant forward and spoke softly. 'I will give you what you gave me. A small chance. A small chance to survive the bus crash.'

Pedro nodded upwards, like a twitch. 'Go on.'

'Russian roulette. You must fire the gun once. Only once. If you survive the shot, you survive the bus crash.'

'Ha, ha, ha, ha. One in six. That's more than a small chance.'

A wry smile spread across Juan's face as he leant further forward. His stomach pushed against the table and blood gushed from his knife wound. 'There are five bullets. One empty chamber.'

Pedro stood up quickly pushing the table over. He threw his hands in the air. 'Shut the fuck up. I'll never do that.'

Juan lifted the table back into place and sat down before turning back to Pedro. 'The choice is yours. You don't have to do it, but you'll be dead in just under two minutes. Your only chance of living is putting the gun to your head and finding the empty chamber.'

Pedro sat back down. He had a plan. 'Okay, give me the gun.'

The man with the eye patch placed five bullets in the gun, span the barrel and closed it up before handing it to Pedro, covered with his other hand.

Pedro took the gun, pointed at Juan and fired. Click, click, click, click, click, click.

135

He slammed the gun down on the table and shouted. 'You put blanks in it.'

Juan continued with quiet assurance. 'Not me Pedro. YOU put blanks in it. I'm not real. I'm in YOUR head. You have thirty seconds left before you die.'

Juan passed the gun back to the man with the eye patch. He loaded five more bullets and span the barrel before handing it to Pedro.

'Fifteen seconds,' Juan said firmly.

'You must be fucking joking if you think I'm putting that gun to my head.' Pedro put the gun down on the table and took two steps back.

'Okay.' Juan shrugged. 'You're gonna die anyway.'

Pedro held up the palms of both hands and turned his head away.

Juan counted. 'Ten, nine.'

Everyone joined in. 'Eight, seven, six, five.'

'No fucking way,' shouted Pedro, his eyes fixed on his own bleeding, unconscious body.

'Four, three, two.'

Pedro dived for the table, grabbed the gun and put it to his temple.

Bang.

15 ... **Or toss a coin**

Five years before the crash, Friday, February 9, 1979: 'Aaaagh.' Costa jumped instinctively back through the door, spilling paint from an open tin. 'Jesus. You nearly gave me a heart attack.'

Geoff Miller fell to his knees laughing. He had been waiting around the corner for five minutes hoping to make Costa jump. He had been reading The Sun during their tea break and a story had given him an idea. A robber in America had wrapped toilet paper around his head as a disguise during a raid on an all-night store. Geoff had been to the toilet and wrapped half a roll of tissue paper around his head, leaving his eyes and mouth exposed and tucked the loose end under his baseball cap.

'You're lucky the carpets are up, otherwise we'd have been buying new ones.'

Geoff carried on laughing.

Costa's eyes narrowed. 'What's the matter with you Geoff? You're one month away from repossession and you're still fooling around.' Costa was angry but he couldn't help a small smile. They had both laughed when Geoff read out The Sun story.

Geoff controlled himself and started unwinding the paper. 'Sorry Costa. You're right.' He'd stopped laughing, but as the tissue came off, he revealed a cheeky smile. 'I hope my tea's not cold. I thought you'd never come. I was waiting ages.'

'Right. You can use that paper to mop up this paint.'

Geoff tidied the mess before sitting back down to finish his lunch.

'Shushhhh,' whistled Geoff, reaching for the radio volume dial.

'Forest have signed Francis. Over a million.'

'Woahhh.' Geoff punched the air. He was a Nottingham Forest fan and Brian Clough had been after Trevor Francis for some time.

'The prolific marksman has signed for Brian Clough's league and cup winning side this lunchtime after eight years at Birmingham City, the first transfer to break the million pound barrier.'

'Result,' shouted Geoff, again punching the air. 'Game over. That makes us favourite to keep the title.'

'Wouldn't be so sure.' A word of caution from Costa. 'I think Liverpool will still do you. Maybe even West Brom.'

'Naah. Walk in the park. Tenner says Forest win the league.' Geoff held out his hand. 'I'll even give you odds.'

Costa refused to shake. 'Will you never learn?'

Geoff frowned and looked a little put out. 'But it's the safest bet in the history of betting.'

Costa rolled his eyes and shook his head. 'Listen Geoff.' Costa paused while Geoff turned the radio down. 'You lost £5,000 of the bank's money on Yellow Submarine. Yes. An excellent horse. And yes. You were unlucky. It pulled up lame in the final furlong.'

'Just unlucky.'

'Okay. Maybe. Then you sold your car and borrowed another £10,000. Lost it all on Eight Days A Week. Unlucky I know. Fell at the final fence, but Geoff, it happens to you all the time.'

'Forest to win the league. Tenner.' Geoff offered his hand again.

'No. I'm not doing it any more.' Costa pushed his hand away. 'I'm not surprised Kez left you. I AM surprised she came back the first time, cleared your mortgage and you land yourself in debt again backing the bloody gee gees. You're a pratt Geoff. And now you're one missed payment away from repossession.'

No reaction from Geoff.

'Jesus Geoff. Get a grip. You keep telling me she'll come home when you hit the jackpot. She doesn't want you to hit the sodding jackpot. She wants you to stop pissing your life down the drain.'

Geoff sank his teeth into a cheese sandwich and looked blankly at the newly painted walls.

Costa wasn't happy with silence. He wanted Geoff to acknowledge his gambling problem. He reached his hand out and rested it on Geoff's shoulder. 'You've got to sort yourself out mate.'

Geoff finished his tea and placed the empty mug by the radio. 'I wish I could play football. A million quid would go a long way.'

'You could run up a tab at the bookies with that much cash in the bank.'

Geoff smiled and nodded. 'Too many bloody pies though. I'm nearly 16 stone now.'

Costa slapped him on the back. 'Your fucked mate. Fat pie-eating gambling addict. Why do I put up with you?'

'Cos I'm a bloody good decorator.' He stood up again, but fell back down in his seat.

'You alright?' asked Costa.

Geoff looked a bit pale. 'Yeah. Think so. Funny pain in both legs though. Just below the knees. Must've sat down too long.'

They both sat quietly as Tragedy by the Bee Gees played in the background.

Geoff sang along. 'When the money's gone and you can't go on, it's tragedy.'

'Stop gambling. Make your next mortgage payment and you'll get out of this mess.' Costa gave Geoff all the right advice but knew he wouldn't take it.

Geoff looked up. 'I hate ceilings. Another cup of tea before we start?'

'Yeah. Go on then.' There was no heating in the house while the decorators were in and it was a cold winter day.

Geoff lay on his back and reached under the sideboard to unplug the kettle. 'Aargh,' he yelped as he banged his elbow. 'Pain in the neck this bloody kettle.'

He filled it in the other room before lying on his back again and reaching under the sideboard. After flicking the switch on, he stayed on the floor and stared into space. 'We could do with an extension lead for this kettle.'

'Yeah. Makes sense,' agreed Costa.

Geoff looked thoughtful despite his vacant stare. 'Better still, somebody should invent a kettle, which doesn't have a lead. If it just had a plug built in underneath, you could plug it direct into the extension lead.'

'Cordless kettle. Nice idea. That could make some money.' Costa nodded approval.

'Better still.' Geoff's idea was evolving. 'How about a cordless mug? You just plug your mug into an extension lead, it boils the water and you drop your teabag in. Job done.'

'I think you've found your vocation Geoff. Inventor to help lazy bastards.' Costa stood up. 'Quick pee.' He headed off to the toilet.

Five minutes later, he hadn't come back and his tea was going cold.

'Costa,' shouted Geoff.

No reply.

'Costa. Tea.'

Nothing.

Geoff finished off the last of his tea, placed his mug next to the radio and went to look for Costa.

'Aaaagh.' Geoff darted back through the door, bumping his elbow again. 'Bastard Costa.'

Costa spat bits of tissue paper all over Geoff as he burst out laughing but then stood quietly.

'Nice job Costa,' Geoff had to admit. 'Just your eyes and mouth showing and the loose ends neatly tucked under your woolly hat.'

Costa didn't reply.

'Come on. We've got a ceiling to paint and you've got a cold cup of tea to drink.'

Geoff pulled Costa's hat off and started unwinding the toilet paper. He felt a little uneasy. Costa said nothing. The bad feeling grew stronger when Geoff exposed grey hair. He stopped for a minute. Costa didn't have grey hair. He unravelled a bit more paper to expose a pasty white forehead. Costa had tanned olive coloured skin. This wasn't Costa. He unwound the rest of the paper slowly. As soon as he uncovered the eyes, he recognised the man. It was his bank manager.

'It's Mr Baines isn't it?'

'No.'

'Yes it is. You're my bank manager, Mr Baines.'

'No. I'm the Grim Reaper.'

'What?' Geoff looked around quickly. 'Where's Costa?'

'He sacked you four years ago when you ran up £5,000 of debts on the partnership's trade account.'

'I've just made him a cup of tea.'

143

'You've just been in a bus crash.'

'Piss off.' Geoff smiled at Mr Baines, but the bon homie faded as he looked around the upturned bus at the ripped metal, twisted seats, twisted bodies and injured passengers.

Mr Baines waited for the gravity of the situation to sink in before he looked beyond Geoff and nodded upwards.

Geoff turned and looked up. His eyes stretched wide open as his head jolted with shock. He saw his own unconscious body hanging from the concertinad seats. Both his legs were trapped, just below the knees. He said nothing. His head was spinning.

Mr Baines pointed towards an upturned milk crate next to a pile of paint tins. 'Have a seat Mr Miller.'

The Grim Reaper sat on another milk crate and again gestured his hand for Geoff to sit down. He did, but still said nothing.

Grim gave him a moment to collect his thoughts.

'I'm dead right?'

'No. But you're in a bad way.'

'Have you come for me then?'

Mr Baines looked Geoff in the eye. His blank expression gave nothing away. 'Maybe. I have a quota of 16 to fill from the people on this bus. You're a strong contender.'

Geoff didn't reply. He covered his face with his hands and a tear welled up in his eye.

Grim looked thoughtful. Almost surprised. 'Talk to me.'

Geoff took his hands away from his face and looked up at Grim, tears flowing a little faster. 'I've thought about dying many times.'

Grim nodded.

'I couldn't have asked for a better wife and I let her down. Not once. Time and time again. And Costa. My best friend. He tried to help me and I stole from him.'

'And what? You thought about taking your own life?'

Geoff sat up straight. 'I did Mr Baines. I certainly bloody did. Nice life insurance policy. See them right. They're both better off without me.'

'And now you face the genuine possibility of death, do you feel the same way?'

'Yes,' Geoff answered without hesitation. 'It tidies all the loose ends. I probably deserve to die.'

'But you're not sure are you?'

'It would be nice to put things right and start again. Make it up to them.' Geoff looked up at his trapped body. 'Am I hurt bad?'

Grim looked at Geoff, then his eyes moved up to the portly decorator's body. 'You're fine apart from your legs. They are crushed. If you get help quick enough, your life can be saved but you will probably lose both legs.'

Geoff smiled. 'Last thing I said to Coyley before we set off was, "Bet you a tenner the flight's delayed." Probably will be now. I'd have won a bet. Yoopy doo.'

Geoff sat back down and thought for a moment before facing Grim again. 'So what is this? Punishment for my gambling problem?'

Mr Baines shook his head. 'No. Could have been anyone. You were just unlucky.'

Geoff laughed. 'Costa always said I was unlucky.' He noticed the Grim Reaper check his watch. 'Oh right. Time's a wasting. What happens now?'

Mr Baines reached into his pocket and pulled out a 50 drachma coin and ran it between his fingers following the coin with his eyes, before looking up at Geoff. 'That's up to you.'

Geoff looked at the coin.

'I'm going to give you a choice.' Grim played with the coin a little more. 'Like I said, if you get help, you'll survive, but you'll lose both legs. We could leave it at that if you want.'

'Or?'

'Or.' The Grim Reaper stared blankly at Geoff. 'Or I toss this coin once. Call it right and you survive the crash with a full recovery. You keep your legs. Call it wrong and you die.'

16 ... **And the pound deal**

A month before the crash, Sunday, March 11, 1984: 'Seven. Go on. Seven.' Peter kissed the dice and rolled. 'Yeahhh,' he shouted with delight as he picked up his small tin battle ship and moved it seven places forward to Vine Street. 'Game over. I am the god of Monopoly.' Peter stood and did a little jig.

John and Sarah Coyle were playing Monopoly with their two kids, Peter, 12, and Chloe, 14. Saturdays were always taken up with John's refereeing duties, so Sunday was family day, but when it rained they played Monopoly. The competition was fierce and nothing pleased John's kids more than beating their property developing dad at a game which he should win every time. Over the years though, they had picked up all his tricks and come up with newer and more creative deals.

This particular game had hinged on Vine Street. John had the other two oranges and Vine Street was his last chance of a set, while Peter and Chloe already had a set each, Chloe the browns and Peter the light blues. Both already had hotels. If Peter could stop his dad getting Vine Street, the game was almost won, as Peter had at least one card from most of the sets. The potential for deals to undermine the boy was limited.

Chloe scowled as Peter landed on Vine Street. Peter had won the last two games and had gloated every day for almost a month, most annoyingly when the two met at school. Humiliating. Firstly because she had a younger brother and secondly because he embarrassed her with his smug chants in front of her friends. It just wasn't cool.

'In yer face Chloe,' shouted Peter as he held up two fifty pound notes and waved them within six inches of her face. 'I'll buy it mortgaged.' All his property, with the exception of the light blues, had been mortgaged to buy hotels.

'Get stuffed,' snapped Chloe, pushing Peter's hand away.

'Steady on,' urged John.

Peter wasn't happy with Chloe's response and he reached close in front of Chloe to pick up the Vine Street card.

'Back off arsehole.' Chloe pushed Peter's arm again.

Sarah pointed a finger towards Chloe. 'Not one of your words Sweety. No need for that.'

Peter held up his arms professing his innocence. 'Never touched her. What a bad loser.'

Chloe's voice shot up an octave as she defended herself facing her mum. 'He was way inside my personal space and he IS an arsehole.' She turned to Peter. 'You're just a sad loser. Just lucky anyway. I'm a much better player. Git.'

John pointed a finger towards Chloe this time. 'Not one of your words Chloe. Pack it in, both of you. This is supposed to be a happy family game. I'm the one that needed Vine Street the most, so you two shouldn't be fighting. You've got the only two sets.'

'Yes Dad. I am aware of that thank-you. But Vine Street still decides the game. Peter's got all the negotiating power now.'

'Not all. Not all the power yet Chloe.' John tried to restore calm.

Peter tried to gloat a little more by holding the Vine Street card towards Chloe's head and flicking her ear.

She punched him on the top of the arm hard enough to stop him smiling and trigger a violent response. He thrust his fist in her direction but she was ready and parried his clenched hand to one side, a glancing blow. She had landed a clean punch so Peter felt he needed to try again, but as he recoiled to strike, he was restrained by his father.

'Oi! What's the matter with you two. If this was a Saturday afternoon, I'd give you both a red card.' John held Peter down in his seat, while pointing at his daughter. 'How many times have I told you? No violence. Nobody wins a fight.' Looking back at his son, he shook his head gently. 'I'm not saying she was right to hit you, but you do ask for it sometimes. Stop winding her up.'

John sat back down and there was a brief moment of truce.

'Okay. Whose go is it?' asked Sarah.

'Must be Dad,' said Chloe, 'Because arsehole just landed on Vine Street.'

Peter's response was to press his forefinger against his thumb just behind Chloe's little tin dog on Fleet Street and flick it halfway across the room.

John was angry now. 'Stop it.' He shouted so loud that droplets of spit flew across the board. 'Just stop it. It's a game. Just a bloody game. It really isn't worth fighting over.' He picked up the dog and put it back on Fleet Street before collecting the dice in his right hand.

He looked from Chloe to Peter and back again with disapproval. He had been splitting up fights between his kids for longer than he could remember and had run out of ideas.

There had been a time when Chloe was only six and Peter four when he had been at his wit's end and taken a daring gamble in a fruitless bid to end the continual feud.

'Right you two. Get your coats on, and your shoes and stand by the back door.'

The fight had stopped for a moment while the two confused children had done as they were asked, both wondering where they were going. Their confusion grew when John met them by the back door with a cricket bat. They both looked at the bat, then at each other. Four-year-old Peter did up the zip on his blue anorak before looking up at his father.

'Where are we going Dad?'

'To the hospital,' John quickly replied with a calm but firm tone.

The children looked at each other still confused.

'Why?' asked Chloe, now just a little anxious.

'To get you both patched up,' replied John, still calm. 'You are both so determined to hurt each other and ignore me and your mum that we may as well get it over with. You will eventually put each other in hospital anyway as you both raise the stakes in your endless fights.'

They still looked unsure.

'So we'll cut out the never-ending battles and skip straight to the big one. I want you to take it in turns to smash each other around the head with the cricket bat until neither of you can stand up. Then I'll drive you both to the hospital.'

Chloe and Peter were lost for words, not sure if their dad meant it. 'Who wants to go first?'

There was no volunteer.

'Okay Chloe. You first.' John handed her the bat. 'Right Peter. Stand still so she gets a good clean strike.'

Chloe held the bat handle loosely allowing the heavy end to rest on the floor. She looked at the fear in Peter's eyes.

'Come on Chloe. Let's get this over with. My telly programme is on soon. You're going to make me miss it. Hit him. Smash his head in. You've been heading that way for weeks. Months. Save us all a lot of grief and hit him.' John lifted the bat above Chloe's shoulder. It was a bizarre gamble for a man whose main ambition was to save another person's life. Inwardly he preyed that his instincts were right. He had no plan B in the event that they actually hit each other.

Chloe held the bat out straight at shoulder height, shaking a little.

John looked into her eyes as they filled with tears. She let the bat drop and looked completely lost, not knowing what to do. She started crying out loud. Peter did the same and they hugged each other. They cried together.

John picked up the bat and left them.

'Go on then Dad. Roll,' urged Chloe.

'When I'm ready,' John replied sternly. 'As you quite correctly pointed out, the game is Peter's. I need to do a deal.' John looked at the properties in front of his wife and two kids. A lot of John's properties were useless without Peter's help and Peter wouldn't trade as he already had the winning hand. The only sets he could complete with Chloe or Sarah's help were the dark blues and the stations.

Chloe was better placed than John, so unlikely to be very helpful, but Sarah had almost nothing he needed. He had very few options. Plenty of property but nothing he could make much money from. His situation in the game was remarkably similar to the problems he was facing in real life.

He still hadn't told Sarah how bad their finances were. He had raced down every morning to get to the post before Sarah, so she didn't see all the red bills. They were a whisker away from having their home repossessed and the electricity would probably be cut off in the next few days.

His only hope was Giles Thornton, chairman of Southside YMCA Football Club, a fellow developer who had secured a contract to build 200 new homes and promised John some sub-contracted work in exchange for a week's work on Giles' Corfu villa.

John had refereed a YMCA cup game before Christmas. Giles had jokingly offered John financial help in exchange for fixing the game. YMCA had won. But they would have won regardless of anything John had done as referee. They were the better side. John had kept away from Giles after the game. But John was desperate and had called Giles before the weekend. John was now anxiously waiting for Giles to give him the nod on the deal, so he could pay his mortgage arrears without Sarah ever knowing how bad things had got.

'Chloe.'

'Yes Dad.'

'Interested in a deal?'

'Maybe. Always prepared to listen.'

'How about you sell me Park Lane?'

'How about you sell me Mayfair? If you have the dark blues, you would be stronger than me. Why would I do that?'

'Okay. How about I give you Mayfair and you never charge me rent on the dark blues?' John paused before adding. 'And the pound deal? If you go out of the game, you must sell me the dark blues for a pound.'

Peter didn't like the sound of that. It would make Chloe stronger than him. 'Hold on Chloe. You would have more income than me but Dad would still have none, so I would put him out and take all his properties which would make me stronger than you again.'

Chloe thought for a moment. 'Okay Dad. I'll do that deal if you do me the pound deal on all your other properties. If you go out, you have to give me everything for a pound.'

Peter liked that even less.

'Just a minute.' Sarah joined the negotiations. 'I'm in this game too. I have an idea. John and Chloe. How about you hold off dealing on the dark blues. We have all four stations between the three of us. If you both give me your stations on a lease so they're still yours, I'll have a set, so I can charge full whack but I'll pass the money on to the freeholder of each station, so we all get full price whenever anybody lands on one.'

'But Pet, we'll just be hurting each other.' John couldn't see how that would damage Peter's grip on the game.

'Okay, free to each other, full price to Peter.'

'I'm happy with that.' Chloe could see that she benefited most from that deal as she only had one station. It helped move her a little closer to Peter's income level and if she could kill off Mum or Dad first, she would get the properties she needed to beat Peter.

'How 'bout you Pet?' Sarah asked John. 'We got a deal?'

Having finally got the kids to stop fighting, John's mind had wandered back to Giles and his real-life financial worries. They had been put to the back of his mind until his desperate situation in the game became so similar to his real problems. His response to

Sarah focussed on the game, but he felt almost as if he was finally giving her the true story he should have shared with her many months ago.

'Sarah. I have no money. I have no sets. I can't develop any of my sites. Peter, to my right, has less property than me, but he has a finger in just about every pie. He has the control. Unless things change, I will be bankrupt before the day ends. If you want a deal on the stations, you have a deal on the stations.'

John rolled the dice and landed on Pall Mall, just beyond Peter's hotels. 'Woahh. I survive. Not beaten me yet boy.' He handed the dice to his wife. 'Right. I need a pee. NO DEALS till I get back.'

The house rule was all deals had to be open so everybody had a fair chance, but there was always a temptation to collude when anybody left the room.

John flushed the toilet, washed his hands and looked at his tired face in the mirror.

'What a loser. I'm a property developer and I can't even beat my own kids at Monopoly,' he said to his own reflection. 'No. Change that. I'm a failed property developer.'

'Wrong attitude,' replied his reflection.

'What the fuck?' John uttered under his breath as he took a double take at his own reflection.

Again his reflection spoke. 'Man up John Coyle. Where's your balls?'

John looked around the bathroom. He quickly opened the door and stared out. Nobody there. He shut the door and looked back at his reflection. He put his finger up to the mirror and ran it down the cold glass. His reflected finger did the same. He jolted his head from side to side. His reflected head did the same.

'Did you just talk to me?' he asked his own image, feeling a little stupid.

'Yes.'

John jumped back again before slowly edging back to the mirror. 'First sign of madness talking to yourself you know,' John told his reflection.

'But you're not.'

'Not what? Mad?'

'No. You're not talking to yourself. I'm not you.'

'Who are you then?'

'I'm the Grim Reaper.'

John laughed and sat down on the edge of the bath wondering if he was having a breakdown.

He collected his thoughts before standing back in front of the sink. He rinsed his face and again looked in the mirror. His reflection patiently looked back.

'The Grim reaper huh?'

'Yes. Look further into the mirror behind me.'

John did as he was asked and breathed in sharply. It was hard to work out what he was looking at, but it wasn't his bathroom. It looked like an upturned train carriage or bus, badly damaged, and there were bodies and suitcases everywhere.

John looked back on his own side of the mirror. He was no longer in his bathroom. He was on the crashed bus.

He looked back at his reflection. 'What do you want? Am I dead?'

'I want you to show some fighting spirit. You're not dead yet. You're unconscious. This bus is half off a cliff and could fall any minute and you are trapped. Two of your fingers have been crushed between your seat and the side of the bus, but if you don't come round soon, you may not get the chance to do anything about it.'

'So how do I come round?'

'Look behind me again.'

Again John did as he was asked. He saw his own bathroom. Looking back on his side of the mirror he was back in his bathroom. In a panic, he looked up at the mirror. 'What do I do?'

'Wake up.'

'How?'

'Can't help you there, but I can tell you, if you go out of the Monopoly game before you wake up, you're dead.'

'Hurry up,' shouted Peter from the other room.

John sat back at the table and nervously counted his money. 'No deals while I was gone?'

'Nothing Pet?' Sarah assured him.

'Okay. Game on.'

'Eight. Eight. Eight.' Peter chanted.

Sarah rolled. Eight.

'Yeahhh,' shouted Peter as Sarah pushed her iron on to Pentonville Road, which was fatal considering she had just landed on Chloe's Old Kent Road.

'£600 please,' demanded Peter.

Sarah scratched around her property cards and few notes. '£200. That's all I've got. Well done Peter.' She gathered her cards and held them out towards Peter.

Chloe and John looked alarmed.

John reached forward and pushed Sarah's hand back. 'Just a minute Mrs Coyle. To be fair to me and Chloe, you have to make a better effort than that to stay in the game.'

'Come on John. I've no chance and I just want to get on with dinner.' She again reached her cards towards Peter.

John again pushed her hand back. 'Sarah. It really isn't fair on me and Chloe and having played for over an hour, you can't choose who wins because you'd rather make tea. Let's talk.'

Sarah frowned deeply. This was all far too serious for a Sunday family bonding session. 'What then John?'

'How about you sell me your properties for £600 and I continue giving you half the rent I get from them?'

Chloe didn't like that. 'Don't do that Mum. He'll only mortgage them, so you'll get nothing and you'll be out anyway. I'll give you £800 for your properties and I'll give you all the rent they earn.' Chloe knew it was a very generous deal, but safe considering her mum would be out soon anyway.'

Peter didn't want the spare properties falling into the hands of his stronger rivals. 'Mum. Give me your station and you don't have to pay anything.'

Sarah wanted to get on with dinner. She reached for John's empty beer bottle and spun it in the middle of the table. It finished pointing at Chloe. She handed Chloe her cards. 'They're yours for £399.' She then handed Peter her £200 and Chloe's £399. 'Couldn't make the payment. I'm out.' She stood and left them to it. As the game went on, Chloe and Peter grew stronger while John steadily lost his money and his properties until he was left with just Mayfair and £75.

Chloe and Peter were equally strong and the game would be decided by who put Dad out. That person would get Mayfair and probably win the game. John rolled and landed on Pentonville.

'Yeahhh,' shouted Peter. 'Game over. I am the god of Monopoly. In yer face Chloe.' Peter stood again for a celebratory jig. 'Dad. I do believe you are out.' He held out his hand to his father. 'Mayfair please.'

Chloe stood up and started walking away.

'Hold on Chloe. Sit back down.'

Chloe turned to face them both. 'Why Dad? He's won. You've nothing left to deal with.'

John thought quickly. The game couldn't end. He would die. 'Sit down Chloe,' he shouted as his mind raced, hunting for ideas. His concentration was broken by a sharp pain in two fingers.

Peter and Chloe were both surprised by their father's determination. Even Sarah had heard the urgency in his voice from the other room and came through to see what was happening.

'Chloe. Would you like to buy Mayfair?'

Peter didn't understand. 'Dad, she's only got £200. You owe me £600. You'd still go out.'

'I know. Chloe. Do you want Mayfair for £1?'

Peter was angry now. 'Course she does Dad. But why? You go out of the game and Chloe wins instead of me. That's not fair. Why would you do that?'

'Because you don't want me to Peter.'

'What a nasty thing to do.'

'£1 Chloe?'

'Yeah. Don't see why not.' She held out one pound.

John reached to take it, but before he did, he turned to Peter. 'I won't do this deal if you agree to accept £1 instead of £600.'

'What's the point in that? You'll never win because you have nothing. All you'll do is keep holding me or Chloe to ransom every time you land on us so nobody can win. What kind of a father does something as desperate as that to his own kids?'

'Deal boy or no?'

'Deal Dad. I've no choice.'

As Chloe rolled the dice, the doorbell rang.

Sarah answered. It was Giles Thornton and a portly man in his mid thirties. After a brief conversation, they came in the room. John stood and shook Giles' hand.

Sarah gave John a questioning look. 'Have you got something to tell me John? Giles says it's all on.'

John threw his arms in the air with delight and shook Giles hand again. 'Excellent Giles. When do I go?'

'April 4 for a week.'

Sarah again looked at John waiting for answers.

'I'm off to Corfu for a week Pet.'

She raised her eyebrows. 'Very nice. I could use a holiday.'

John grimaced. 'Sorry Pet. Just me. Working on Giles' villa.'

Giles corrected them both. 'Actually John. You won't be on your own. I've got you a decorator to help speed the work along.' Giles turned towards the portly man. 'This is

Geoff Miller.' He turned back towards John.
'And Geoff, this is John Coyle.'

John took a step forward and reached out
his hand.

Geoff smiled warmly but instead of
shaking John's hand, he raised his own hand
higher and slapped John around the face.
Chloe and Peter looked startled.

'Just a minute,' shouted Sarah reaching
to help her husband.

Giles was too surprised to do anything at
first but Geoff carried on. He slapped John
repeatedly around the face.

John was so shocked himself that he
slumped to his knees and reached for the wall
to steady himself. He shut his eyes and there
was a ringing in his ears.

Geoff carried on slapping him around the
face and shouting at him. 'John. John. John.
Wake up.'

John slowly opened his eyes. His vision
was blurred. He couldn't tell where he was
but the pain in his fingers was intense. His
head was throbbing and his chest felt
stretched. As his vision cleared, he started to
fill in the blanks. He was suspended from his
fingers upside down in the wreck of a bus.
Geoff Miller, his decorator, was also trapped
in the seat next to him. He saw the sea out of

the smashed back window of the bus and he could feel the gentle movement of the swaying bus as it teetered on the edge of the cliff.

'John mate. If we don't get out quick we're dead.'

17 ... **Miss Corfu**

Day before the crash, Wednesday, April 11, 1984: Miss Corfu contestant number six walked slowly down the stairs of the Socrates Plaza in Sidari as contestant number fourteen walked up. They stopped in front of each other on the half landing as the palm-lined stairs turned through 90 degrees. They both wore short black cocktail dresses, stiletto shoes and long gold earrings. Six had a cotton dress while Fourteen's was a shiny black satin fabric which caught the low evening sun streaming in through the glass doors of the hotel foyer.

Most of the staff and guests were in the main conference room for the Miss Corfu pageant, but Six and Fourteen had nipped out for a costume change. Spiros Gekas was one of the judges and he had left briefly for a toilet break.

As he turned to climb the stairs, he stopped dead in his tracks, mouth wide open as he looked up at the two beauties above him on the turn of the stairs. They hadn't noticed him. Six leant back slightly with both arms behind her resting on the wrought iron stair rail, while Fourteen faced her, their bodies almost touching. Fourteen reached forward and placed her hands on the other girl's hips.

Their faces were only inches apart. Six looked coyly into the other girl's eyes before looking down at her cleavage. Fourteen bit her lip gently as she edged closer to the other girl, at the same time running her hand down Six's hip to her thigh. As they were about to kiss, Spiros dropped his keys and they both pulled away from each other.

'Girls.' Spiros picked up his keys and headed up the stairs. 'Sorry I disturbed you.'

Six and Fourteen smiled as they realised they had been caught out by one of the judges. They looked at each other, plotting silently before looking back at Spiros.

'That's okay,' Six reassured Spiros.

'Actually,' added Fourteen, 'We have a couple of minutes. Join us for a quick drink on our balcony.'

They stood either side of Spiros, took an arm each and led him up the stairs, along the marble corridor and into a large hotel bedroom, with an equally large secluded balcony overlooking the bay.

Fourteen frowned. 'It's so hot in these rooms,' she said as she pulled her dress up over her head.'

Spiros was lost for words as his eyes danced all over her tanned body. Her burgundy lingerie left very little to Spiros' imagination. He faced the other girl expectantly. She didn't disappoint him as she pulled down the zip at the back of her dress, pushed the straps forward and let the black cotton garment fall to her feet.

'One of us will get the drinks, while the other helps you judge the contest,' said Six, as she sat next to Spiros and draped her arms around his neck.

'Sounds good to me.' Spiros undid his shirt buttons.

'Who would you like to get the drinks?'

'Don't mind.' Spiros thought they were both stunning.

'You have to say. Six or Fourteen.'

Spiros shook his head. He really didn't care.

'Choose now,' shouted Six with great urgency.

'Errr Six,' stammered Spiros.

'Louder,' pushed the girl.

'Six,' said Spiros firmly.

'Louder,' she insisted.

'Six,' shouted Spiros. 'Six.'

'Six what?' asked Elaine White, Spiros' mistress, as she shook his shoulders gently to wake him.

Spiros sat up straight, his head spinning as he untangled the dream from the reality of his parked bus. He had fallen asleep in the big Sidari car park behind the Socrates Plaza hotel.

'Err. Six. Our meeting is at six in Joe's.'

'Yes. And we're late. Come on.'

They wandered through the alleyway, which ran down the side of the Socrates from the car park to the main street and crossed the road to Joe's British Bar. It was very busy. Elaine's holiday company had gathered all its reps and associated staff, including the transfer bus drivers, for a meeting to discuss the coming season. Joe's wife Sonia greeted them both with a kiss and pointed to a table of drinks.

'Here we go again.' Sonia rolled her eyes. She loved Corfu, but didn't enjoy running around after drunken tourists.

'I'm looking forward to it actually. It's been a quiet winter. I'll just nip to the ladies before the meeting starts.' Elaine hurried away.

'The bus is full of petrol, my bags are packed and I'm ready to drive you away from all this Sonia. We would be so good together.' Spiros smiled as he reached his arm around her waist and pulled her closer.

'Spiros, you're unbelievable.' Sonia pushed him away. 'Elaine will be back any second.'

'You know you're my favourite.' Spiros winked at her.

'You really need to be more careful.' Sonia didn't know why she was helping him. He certainly didn't deserve it. 'I saw your wife in the supermarket earlier. She may still be in town.'

Spiros quickly looked towards the high street, then back towards Sonia just as Elaine returned with two glasses of wine.

'Thanks Babe.'

'What you looking for?' Elaine asked looking beyond them towards the high street.

'Nothin' Babe.' He reached for Elaine's hand, kissed her on the cheek and led her to a table at the back ready for the meeting.

Thirty minutes later they applauded Greg, the company's regional director, who invited questions.

A little boy near the front put his hand in the air. Nobody seemed surprised that a boy of about six years old had attended the meeting and Greg faced him to take the question.

'Go ahead, young man.'

Colin Gekas stood up and looked across at his father Spiros, before turning back to the regional director. 'Please sir. What would you do if your father was cheating on your mother?'

Spiros had been taking very little notice of Greg and his ambitious plans for the new season, but as soon as he heard his son's voice, he was alert. He stared with disbelief at his eldest child and released his grip on Elaine's hand.

The fair-haired, blue-eyed boy stood patiently waiting for his answer.

Greg thought for a moment and answered as sincerely as if the boy were one of his key staff members. 'You would have to consider whether the disruption to family life were effecting your father's work life. I can only concern myself with how private matters impact on the economic targets of the company.'

'That sounds like flippant commercial jargon to me. I was hoping for a more considered answer which demonstrates a commitment to your staff beyond the working day.'

Colin Gekas was only six years old, but his carefully constructed sentences didn't cause a single raised eyebrow among the assembled reps.

Greg had no answer. He turned away from the boy. 'Let me pass that question to the floor. Any suggestions?'

There was a brief silence before the phone rang behind the bar. Sonia answered before waving over to Spiros. He took the call as Elaine offered Greg her suggestion.

'Maybe the boy should speak to his father. If he could understand why his father were behaving badly, it might help their relationship.' She looked around at her nodding colleagues. 'That can only be of benefit to the company. Happy workers … happy holiday-makers.'

Greg looked towards Colin.

Colin looked towards his father on the bar phone.

'Why are you calling me here?' Spiros asked Iokaste.

'I can see you.'

Spiros looked across the high street and along to the chip shop. Iokaste waved from behind the counter.

'You told me she meant nothing to you. I can see you holding her hand from here.'

'You know I'd rather be with you. I'm keeping up appearances. I'll lose my job if I don't.' Spiros looked across at where Colin had been but he had gone. 'I told you. Elaine means nothing to me. As soon as you finish tonight, I'll be round. I have a present for you. Can't wait to see you in it.'

Spiros had nothing but hoped the thought of gifts would keep Iokaste happy. He hung up and turned back towards Elaine. Colin had sat with her.

'Fuck it,' Spiros said quietly, although it was a little louder than he intended and a couple of girls on the nearest table gave him a look. He disappeared off to the relative safety of the gents.

By the time he regained his composure and returned to the veranda bar, the meeting had finished. Most of the reps had stayed for a drink and to share stories of winter back home, while a few Greeks had dropped by to renew old friendships.

But for Spiros, things were going from bad to worse. Elaine was sat with his son

Colin and Sonia, and they had been joined by Spiros' wife Clara and his other two children. The two-year-old was crying and Clara was trying to pacify her with a glass of lemonade.

They were all enjoying light-hearted small-talk. Spiros was confident that he was safe for the moment. He considered nipping across the road for chips, but Colin saw him. They held eye contact for a few seconds before the boy started shaking his head slowly.

The women hadn't seen him, so he skirted the edge of the bar in a bid for the safety of the street.

'Oi Dad,' shouted Colin.

His women all looked across at him.

Spiros stopped for a fraction of a second, before reaching down to pick up an imaginary coin. He then changed direction and joined the others.

'Dropped a coin,' explained Spiros. 'Almost rolled out to the street.'

Sonia forced a smile. 'Your boss?' she asked.

'What?' Spiros looked confused.

'On the phone?'

'Ah. Yes. My boss.'

Elaine was about to push Spiros for introductions.

Clara was about to ask Spiros what he wanted for tea.

Sonia, the only other person apart from Spiros, who knew who everybody was, came to his rescue.

'We must clear out the old stock ready for the new season. How about a free ice cream kids?'

Their faces lit up.

'Spiros, do me a favour will you? Take them to the cooler for an ice cream while you're up.'

'Sure. This way.' He headed off.

Elaine watched them reach for Spiros' hand and thought to herself how sweet it looked. Spiros would make an excellent father. He was obviously very good with children.

'Elaine.' Sonia reached her arm towards Spiros' wife. 'This is Clara. She was a rep many years ago. Loved it so much she stayed.'

They gently shook each other's hands.

'Clara. This is Elaine. Second season on the island. I think you may both be from the same part of England.' Sonia had no idea where they were from but hoped she could start a conversation unrelated to Spiros, between his wife and mistress.

Colin pointed to a strawberry Cornetto pictured on the side of the cooler. Spiros reached inside and grabbed a mint Cornetto and handed it to Colin without looking at him. He was looking beyond him at his wife and mistress deep in conversation.

Colin handed the ice cream back. 'Strawberry Dad. I said strawberry. I know they're all nice, but unlike you, I know exactly which one I want.'

The hint of cheek distracted Spiros from his women and he turned to face his son. 'Strawberry? Okay.' He looked deep into the cooler and pulled out a strawberry Cornetto. He turned to hand the ice cream to Colin, but he was gone. There was a man stood where Colin had been.

Spiros looked past him for his son, but couldn't see him.

'You seen a small boy mister? Fair hair, blue eyes'

The man, in his early twenties wore tight jeans, brightly polished black shoes and a black dress shirt open at the collar. His hair was gelled back and he wore a heavy gold chain around his neck. When he reached up to remove his mirrored sunglasses, Spiros noticed his striking blue eyes.

He swallowed. His mouth instantly felt dry. His first thought when he saw this man was disgust. What's this greasy arrogant charmer doing in Joe's Bar? But as soon as he saw the eyes, he saw himself. The clothes, the swagger, the cocky smile. This was Colin as a young man. He had copied everything that was bad in his father.

'You are Colin aren't you?

'No. No I'm not.'

'You ARE. You are my son?'

'No. I'm the Grim Reaper. And I don't like you. In fact, for you, I'm going to break my own rules and change my mind. Your unborn child deserves to live more than you and your family will be better off without you.'

'What are you talking about?'

'You're coming with me.'

Spiros looked back towards Elaine, but she was no longer at the table, instead, she lay unconscious on the floor. He looked back towards the bar. It was blurred. He could not distinguish what the other customers were doing. He shook his head. He felt faint. He looked back towards the glass front of the cooler.

Beyond the glass there were no ice creams. Instead he saw a road. An empty road. He felt as if he could pass out at any moment but he fought the feeling and focussed on the road. There was a van coming. It stopped and a man jumped out with great urgency. He knew him. It was Ilias from the bar in Avliotes.

18 ... **It can stay a secret**

Day of the crash, Wednesday, April 11, 1984:
'Where's the shoebox?' Keres asked Thanatos with surprise in her voice.

Thanatos put his coffee down on the round plastic table and leant back in his seat looking up at the peach umbrella. 'I changed my mind Keres.'

'Yeahhh.' Keres couldn't hide her joy as she punched the air. But the celebration stopped for a moment. She wanted to know who the Grim Reaper had taken instead of Elaine White's unborn baby.

Thanatos answered before she asked the question. 'Spiros. The driver.'

'Yeahhh.'

He would have been her choice. She couldn't stop smiling as she finished her coffee and looked along the line of round tables.

The far table with the light blue umbrella was taken by the noisy stag party; Twig, Rozzer, Marco and Dean.

Next to them at the table with the pale yellow umbrella, Sally Whisper's mum and dad sat opposite two empty chairs.

At the lilac table, sisters Jane and Mabel Chimera were arguing bitterly, watched by the murderer Pedro Raphael. There was one empty seat.

The fourth table with the peach umbrella would be empty when their coffee break was over. The shoebox had gone but would later be replaced by the bus driver. Keres counted the empty seats. 'You'd better get busy Thanatos. You still have six seats to fill.'

'No hurry,' Thanatos said calmly, clasping both hands behind his head as a pillow. 'I'm not sure who to sort out next.'

'Who's it between?' asked Hypnos.

Thanatos looked across at the smoking wreck of the bus. 'I need six.' He raised his finger. 'Mind you, it will be hard to stay on target if the bus falls.'

'Go on then. Which six?' Keres asked.

'Well. There are three more people sat in seats I randomly chose before they got on the bus.'

'And?'

'And two more I have in mind but I don't know about the last one.' Thanatos screwed his face up. 'Got a funny feeling about number 16.'

Keres raised her eyebrows. 'Okay. What about the two you have in mind already?'

Thanatos leant forward decisively and rested his elbows on the table. 'I should do them next. They're both married couples.' He rested his hand on the table and tapped his fingers impatiently waiting for inspiration. 'There's a couple in their early sixties. Gordon and Mary. Lovely couple. Got to take one of them though. They've been on my list a few times already. Can't keep letting them both off the hook.' Thanatos tapped his fingers some more. 'But the other couple! Not so easy.'

'Problem shared is a problem halved.' Hypnos was always ready to help with ideas.

'Roy and Daisy Farrell.'

Hypnos and Keres nodded.

'Early fifties. He's a lovely bloke, but, to be honest, she's a bitch. I spoke to her because I wasn't sure if she was as unpleasant as I thought.'

'And was she?' asked Hypnos.

'Yes. Worse actually.'

'Ooh. Let me take care of her then.'
Keres had only dealt with noisy stag guest
Rozzer and Pedro the murderer.

'No. You know I can't do that. Got to be
a bit random.'

Keres slouched back in her seat.

'I think I'll give him the choice.'

'But if he's such a nice bloke, he'll let
her live.' Hypnos couldn't help feeling that
the random rule would be broken if his
brother knew what the outcome of a choice
would be.

'Well actually, he may not choose to
save her.'

Hypnos and Keres leant forward.

'Thing is.' Thanatos raised one eyebrow.
'He will die of cancer in about five years if he
survives the bus crash, but she will live
another 30 years.'

'Don't tell him that,' Keres said, a little
louder than intended.

'I won't. But maybe I should.'

'No. Not relevant.' Hypnos shook his
head.

'But I will tell him about his wife's
guilty secret.'

'Ooh. Go on,' urged Keres.

'Roy and Daisy have a 26-year-old son
called Frank. Only child.' Thanatos paused.

Keres held out her hands to usher him on.

'Roy is not the father.'

Keres sat back in her seat.

'And,' added Thanatos. 'She has never told Roy. He thinks Frank is his boy.'

'Result,' said Keres with complete satisfaction.

'Hmm. Not so sure.' Hypnos wasn't convinced. 'If Roy's such a nice bloke. He may forgive her and still let her live.'

'Maybe. Who knows? Anyway, one of them must die and I'm telling Roy his wife's secret and giving him the choice of who lives.'

Keres rubbed her hands together and smiled.

Thanatos looked at his watch and walked towards the bus, just as a van screeched to a halt and Ilias Vyntra started to jump out, but froze as Thanatos stopped time.

Roy Farrell waved the waiter over. 'Could we have another bottle of wine please?'

'Certainly sir.' The waiter turned to leave.

'Oh. And could you light these candles please?'

The waiter turned back, pulled a lighter from his pocket and lit both candles, one in front of Roy and one in front of Daisy. He headed off for the wine.

'Shouldn't have to ask them to light the bloody candles.' Daisy wasn't happy. 'Everyone else's are already lit.' She tutted before tucking into her lamb souvlaki.

Roy took a sip of his wine. 'What was it then?'

'What was what?'

'You were going to tell me something before we ordered more wine.'

'Oh yes.' Daisy reached for her handbag. 'Finished my book this afternoon.'

'Blimey.' Roy was shocked. 'The one you've had sat on the shelf for ten years?'

'Yep. The same.'

'Never thought you'd finish that.' Roy nodded approval. 'Any good?'

'No. It was rubbish.'

'Oh dear.'

'But when I got to the end, I found an old photo, which I tucked away.'

'What? Ten years ago?'

'Yeah.'

'What of?'

Daisy reached into her handbag and passed Roy the photo.

Roy smiled with pride and a tear started to form. 'Bloody hell Daisy. The old Vespa moped. Frank's sixteenth birthday. He loved that bike.'

'Yeah. You spent hours trying to get it working between you.'

Roy's mind wandered with nostalgia as he soaked up the detail in the picture. The left hand side of the bike was a slightly different blue than the right. They had run out of paint and used what was left from another job. There was a crack in the glass of the headlight. Roy had bumped the bike into a tree while showing Frank his off-road skills in the back garden. The road tyres hadn't given him enough grip on the soggy grass through the orchard.

'Sold it didn't he?' Daisy's question brought Roy back to the Sidari restaurant.

'Yes,' nodded Roy. 'To pay for his first car.' Roy leant the photo against a vase in the middle of the table and returned to his beef stifado.

'This bloody wine's awful.' Daisy stood up. 'Goin' right through me.' She headed for the ladies.

The waiter sat in her empty seat.

Roy was about to put a forkful of food in his mouth but stopped mid-air, surprised that a waiter had the audacity to take his wife's seat.

'I need a quick word.'

Roy wasn't sure whether he was in a position to complain. Waiters certainly didn't sit with you at home, but he was in Corfu. Maybe things were different in Greece.

'Okay. How can I help?' Roy stammered. 'I'll have beer if you're out of wine.'

'No. No. I'm not the waiter.'

'You served our food.' Roy was uncomfortable and shuffled a little in his seat.

'Yes. I did. But I'm not a waiter.'

'Who are you then?'

'I'm the Grim Reaper.'

Roy said nothing and his blank expression didn't change. He wasn't sure if the waiter was joking.

After a brief pause, Roy replied. 'Err. I don't understand. I thought you were the waiter. All I wanted was a quiet meal with my wife. We've had a lovely holiday and we ...'

Grim held up his hand and stopped Roy. 'Look around.'

Roy's eyes opened wide with horror as he looked around the wreck of the upturned bus. He started to shake and mumble incoherently, as his eyes twitched around the chaos.

Grim grabbed him by the shoulders. 'Look at me.'

Roy couldn't take it all in and his breathing quickened.

'Look at me Roy.'

Grim finally got his attention, but firmly held his grip on Roy's shoulders.

'You're not dead.'

'What about Daisy? How's Daisy?'

Grim looked towards the front of the bus. 'She's having an asthma attack.'

Roy tried to stand up. 'I've got to get her inhaler.'

'Sit down.' Grim held Roy in his seat. 'Look Roy. Nobody is moving. Time has been stopped. There's no panic. Just listen to me.'

Roy settled a little.

'You can't get her inhaler, but her attack may pass as the air clears.'

'Where's her inhaler?'

'Put the inhaler out of your mind.' Grim spoke with as much authority as he could muster. He wanted Roy to calm down. He had a tough decision to make. 'The inhaler is towards the back of the bus. The bus is balanced on the edge of a cliff. If you go for the inhaler, you could kill everyone.'

'What then?' Roy's trembling had eased.

'Listen carefully.' Grim waited for Roy to compose himself. 'I have a quota to fill and I need you or Daisy to come with me. One of you must die.'

Roy nodded slowly. 'Am I hurt?'

'You've had a few bad knocks. Nothing fatal on it's own, but you have a blood clot heading towards your heart. It could kill you.'

Roy stared into the distance as he weighed it all up. 'So the blood clot might kill me and Daisy's asthma attack could kill her?'

'That sounds about right.'

'Could we both die?'

'It's possible. But I only need one of you.'

'When will we find out?'

'It's not like that. It's not been decided yet.'

'Will you decide?'

'I could, but I want you to make the choice.'

Roy was silent.

Grim waited patiently.

'Okay.' Roy's blank stare ended and he looked back at Grim with purpose. 'Take me.

Daisy deserves to live. She is a good wife and excellent mother.' Roy nodded decisively.

Grim raised his eyebrows in a manner, which invited Roy to reconsider.

'What's wrong? You said I could choose.'

'Yes I did, but before you make your choice, I'd just like you to have another think about Daisy. She's not as good a wife and mother as you …'

It was Roy's turn to stop Grim. 'Doesn't matter.' Roy shook his head. 'Doesn't matter. I know what you're going to say. Frank's not my son and she never told me.'

It was Grim's turn to look surprised.

Roy answered the question Grim was thinking.

'I knew before Frank was born.'

'And you said nothing?'

'What good would that have done?' Roy's voice went up an octave.

Grim had no answer.

'It would have torn us apart. Besides, I loved her. I still do and I see Frank as my own. Frank sees me as his real father. That could never have happened if she had told the truth. She must have felt an awful lot of guilt and she could have unburdened that guilt on me. She never did. So I stand by what I said.

She's a good wife to me and an excellent mother to Frank.'

Things weren't going to plan, but Grim wanted to give Roy one last chance to change his mind.

'Okay. Tell you what Roy. The choice stays with you. One of you must die … or both … I'd take both if you choose it. But I'll give you 30 seconds from when Daisy sits back down to make your choice.'

'And where will you be?'

'Don't worry about that. I'll have gone.'

Roy nodded.

'There is a candle in front of you and another in front of Daisy. Blow one of them out before 30 seconds has passed.'

Roy stared into his food then looked up at Grim. 'Candle out. Dead?'

Grim nodded.

Roy looked back at his food .

Daisy sat down. 'Bastards have run out of toilet paper as well. We should have gone to the Socrates Plaza.' She drank more wine … not an easy thing to do while shaking her head with disapproval.

Roy reached across to hold her hand. 'Daisy.'

The unexpected affection stopped her rant fleetingly, but she quickly resumed.

189

'Where's the wine you ordered? Hope they don't expect a tip tonight.'

'Daisy.'

'No wine. No toilet paper.' She prodded her food. 'And I can't be certain this is lamb. Could be donkey.' The head shaking and tutting was building.

Another customer opened the front door and a gust of wind nearly blew out Daisy's candle. 'No,' shouted Roy with fear in his voice.

Daisy's tantrum came to an abrupt end as the flame on her candle stopped flickering and burned bright. She sat still waiting for an explanation from Roy.

'Daisy.'

'What is it Roy? Spit it out.'

'You have made my life worth living. You have given me a son to be proud of and I will treasure our memories for ever.'

'You alright Roy? Had a knock on the head?' Daisy screwed up her face.

'Daisy. I love you.'

Roy leant forward and blew out his own candle.

19 ... **Trapped**

Minutes after the crash, Wednesday, April 11, 1984: John Coyle kept telling himself not to panic. His head throbbed with blood. As his vision cleared, he took it all in. The bus was upside down. Geoff Miller was upside down. The seat in front was crushing Geoff's legs. His own were restrained but he could move them. They had been held tight enough to stop him falling completely although his two trapped fingers together with his wedged legs pinioned him in a sagged upside down seated position.

'Don't panic John. Don't panic. You're no fucking use to anyone unless you get a grip,' he told himself, but it took all his effort not to pass out. The pain in his hand was intense.

'I can't move mate.' Geoff looked bloated as his face turned deep red with blood.

'How long have I been out?'

''bout five minutes.'

'What happened?' John had to shout over the screams.

'Bus rolled. We're half off the cliff.'

'Anyone got out yet?'

'No way out. Door's jammed.'

John screwed up his face and rubbed his mouth with his free hand. His eyes raced over the debris. 'Gotta think.'

'No fuckin' time to think Coyle. We gotta get out. Bloke up front moved back and the whole bus tipped. Nearly went off the fuckin' cliff till he turned back.'

John raised his eyebrows in submission. 'As soon as the first person steps off then, the rest go over with the bus.'

'Yep.'

'Gotta do something quick.' As soon as he said it he thought, 'Prick John, stating the bleeding obvious whilst unable to move isn't much help.'

He tugged at his trapped hand and tried to lever the twisted wreckage away to release himself but there was no give at all. He had almost resigned himself to a passive role of 'just another victim waiting to be rescued' rather than 'the heroic saviour' of countless members of the first group when the stakes were raised.

'Shit Geoff. Did you hear that?'

'Sort of like a poof?'

'Yeah.'

'Yeah. I heard it. Felt it as well. What was it?'

'Hopefully not what I was thinking.'

Geoff waited for more.

'Sounded like a fire starting.'

Geoff lost his composure and started lashing out at the seat in front to break free.

A wave of fear swept through the bus as they all realised fire had broken out at the front of the bus.

John pulled on his fingers with all his strength and yelled with pain as he felt tissue rip and tear.

He started to drift into semi-consciousness and saw his wife sat in the lounge reading the front page of The Southside Gazette.

'Bus crash kills 49 ... Popular Southside referee John Coyle, who dreamed of saving lives, was one of 49 killed when their bus plunged 300 feet off a cliff in Corfu.'

It had been different in his dreams.

'Swift action helps 49 cheat death ... Popular Southside referee John Coyle dragged 48 others out of the burning wreck of their bus before it crashed down a 300 foot cliff in Corfu.'

A smashing sound cleared his head.

'What was that Geoff?'

'Cavalry's here.' Geoff pointed to the front of the bus. 'Some bloke trying to smash the windscreen.'

'NO!' shouted John. Desperate.

John Coyle was getting angry with himself. 'Focus you twat. Stop dreaming about headlines and fucking do something.' He had to get free. His fingers were stuck. He wasn't going to release them and didn't have time to wait for help. There was only one way forward.

He had to cut them off.

'Geoff.'

His eyes were shut. John shook him. 'GEOFF.'

'Kes. Don't leave me. I can change.'

'Geoff.' John shook him harder. 'Geoff. Help me. We have to get out.'

Geoff tried to focus.

'Come on Geoff. Have you seen my tools? I need my secateurs.'

Ilias Vyntra skidded to a halt. He pulled on the hand-brake while throwing the door open, then lunged into the road and raced to the bus door.

It was jammed up against rocks and shrubs. He climbed over them to get the full picture. It wasn't good. The bus was upside down with its back end thrust dangerously over the edge of the cliff. The side door was too near the back to be any use. It was beyond the edge of the cliff with a three hundred foot drop sucking at it.

One side of the bus was pressed into the shrubs and rocks while the other side was clear ground but none of the side windows had broken. He ran back to his van and pulled open the back doors, grabbed his wheel jack and rushed back to the front of the bus. He would smash the windscreen and help the survivors out.

'Move back,' he shouted, but none of the passengers knew Greek.

Ilias knew no English and urged them back with hand signals.

They edged back and Ilias took a swing. The window starred but didn't break. The passengers saw what he was doing and moved a little further back as Ilias took a second swing. The glass started to craze and a small hole appeared at the point of impact. He could still see through in places but stopped before he took another swing as he heard one of the passengers scream 'NO'.

He took a step back and noticed the front of the bus lift a fraction.

He had a feeling that things were not quite right but knew speed was vital and he prepared to take another swing before a couple of passengers moved back a little more and he noticed the front of the bus lift a little more.

He dropped the jack and ran back to his van in a moment of clarity. The bus was delicately balanced. The slightest movement of passengers towards the back of the bus was tipping it further over the edge. If he broke the screen, as soon as people started escaping, the bus would become heavier at the back and fall.

His brother George had insisted he keep a tow rope in the van and finally he had good reason to be thankful. He hooked it on the back of his van, wrapped it twice round a small tree and tied the other end to the front bumper of the bus.

Then he picked up the jack and finished smashing through the windscreen. Passengers started pushing past him while he was still kicking the broken glass out of their way.

Now his attention was drawn to the flames licking up from the engine, only a few feet above the window the passengers were climbing through.

He had no water in the van and no fire extinguisher. He could do nothing.

As he climbed the lower branch of the small tree which he had used to secure the rope to get a better look, a scooter came round the bend from Palaiokastritsa. A young man jumped off and ran to help people off the bus.

'Go and ring for help,' shouted Ilias.

The young man looked up the tree.

'The bus is going to fall. Go for help.'

He didn't argue. Jumped back on his scooter and sped back down the hill, looking back only briefly when there was a loud screech as the bus started to tilt a little more before sliding inch by inch over the cliff. The rope tightened and Ilias nearly fell out of the tree as he felt it bend out towards the bus.

There was a high-pitched sound of splitting wood, but it stopped as the bus came to rest once more on an outcrop of rock. It gently swayed back and forth as the last few able bodied survivors clambered out through the window.

From his tree, Ilias could see that the fire was on the underside of the engine. There was thick blue smoke. It must be engine oil, but at some point it would find the fuel pipe and work its way along to the tank at the back of the bus. An explosion would not only kill those left on the bus but probably many of those who had left the burning coach.

20 ... **Time's up**

Day before the crash, Tuesday, April 10, 1984: 'Bloody hell Gordon. Look at that.' Mary pointed accusingly at a young man coming down the road on a moped.

Gordon swung round and his eyes widened as the bike approached. 'What an idiot.' He stood and beckoned over the waiter, who was equally taken aback. 'You have to call the police.'

The tired old moped wheezed along the coast road under the terrace of the Athena Taverna in San Stefanos, where Gordon and Mary were enjoying a meal on their last night in Corfu.

A narrow length of rope was tied to the seat of the bike. It was tethered at the other end to a yellow plastic drinks crate. A small toddler, not much more than a baby sat in the crate blissfully unaware of the danger as it scraped along the Tarmac.

'That is unbelievable Mary.'

She shook her head.

'Hit a bump and the crate tips. Fool. Utter fool.' He shook his head. 'Some people should never be allowed kids.'

Mary shook her head a little more as she poured another glass of wine from her carafe.

Gordon tutted, then sipped on his ice cold Mythos. His gaze was fixed on the empty road where the crate had slid by.

They said nothing. Aghast at what they had seen.

A thought bubbled up in Gordon's mind, dislodged by the baby in the crate. 'Mary. I know what I was going to tell you.'

She swallowed her mouthful of Corfiot wine, not the nicest she had ever tasted, but she liked the place and had a when-in-Rome approach to wine selection.

'Jane's daughter did the same as you.'

Mary was lost and tried to follow Gordon's line of thought. The only Jane I know is our neighbour at home. Her with the pregnant daughter. Same as me? What did I do when I was pregnant? Dunno. She needed Gordon to elaborate but he wasn't going to without prompting. She could see him watching her struggle. He always did. It amused him. 'Same as me?'

'You know. Lost one. Found one.'

That didn't help. Still no idea. 'One what?'

'Baby,' he answered in a way which sounded more like, 'Baby you numpty. What else?' He could see she still wasn't with him. 'I don't mean when our Nigel was born. I mean when your mum was pregnant with you. Thought she'd miscarried and lost her baby, but found out that although she had lost one baby, there was still a twin, which she never knew about in the first place.'

Mary smiled. 'Blimey. Jane's daughter was going to have twins. Blimey indeed.'

'I know,' replied Gordon.

'She didn't even want ONE really. Let alone two. What with three kids already ... All under the age of six. Twins would have finished her off. Poor girl. Still, can't be nice losing one.'

'Quite common though, they told her. Happens all the time.'

The food arrived, steam rising off their sizzling hot lamb moussaka. Gordon ran his knife through the top layer to help it cool, took another mouthful of beer, then sat looking at Mary.

She took small fork-fulls of food, blowing on them first, before she felt his eyes on her. She looked up. 'What?'

'Oh. Nothing,' he said softly, dismissively.

'What Gordon? You're clearly deep in thought and your mind is a long way from moussaka.'

He had been thinking about Mary's unborn twin. Would it have been a brother, a sister? If it had been a sister, would it have been identical? Then he thought about whether he might have married the identical sister. His mind flickered about randomly beyond that point as bizarre images of marrying two Marys competed with carnal scenes of threesomes and acts of depravity he had only ever heard about from lewd friends.

'Gordon,' almost sharp but not quite.

'Oh. Nothing really. Just wondered if you ever thought about your twin. You know. What might have happened if she, he, it had been born.'

'No. Not really,' Mary replied quickly.

They both sat in silence staring blankly at the distant olive groves on the hillside up the valley deep in thought.

Gordon had moved on from lascivious thoughts to their only son Nigel. For years they had tried for a second child. At first it had made them closer as they shared the disappointment, but as time passed they found themselves blaming each other and picking fights for no reason. Another house move had almost led to a split.

'I've had enough Gordon. That dentist chair is going to the tip. I hate it. We saved ages for our three piece, I made the curtains to match it, new carpet, hours decorating to match. Hours Gordon. And you want that heap of shit right in the middle.'

She stomped off to the kitchen in a rage, rested both hands on the edge of the sink, sighed deeply then stomped back.

'Right Gordon. You're goin' to have to choose. It's me or the chair.'

Gordon looked lovingly at his favourite chair, then scowled at Mary. 'I had that chair before I met you. It was the first item of furniture I ever owned. Bought it at auction. Roman Road. Southside. That chair and a framed picture of an elephant.'

'Oh Jesus.' Mary tutted. She had hated the elephant picture as well and that had been relegated to the attic years ago.

'I'm serious Gordon, I'm at my wits' end. It really is me or the chair.'

They looked at each other, Mary determined, Gordon feeling helpless. He knew the chair wasn't the problem. It was like so many times before. Mary just wanted to take her anger out on him. Nigel was 12 years old. She wanted a baby. The hospital tests had shown nothing wrong with either of them. They had tried every trick from every book they could find. Nothing worked.

And every time they argued about anything, the worse thing Gordon could do was bring up the baby, but it was always there. It was unavoidable.

He braced himself and took a deep breath.

'Mary.'

She looked him fiercely in the eye, just daring him to speak. 'You mention babies and I'll burn your chair.' And to add strength, 'With you in it.'

He reached for her hand. She yanked it away. 'Don't start that patronising shit. This is nothing to do with babies. I hate your chair.'

He reached for her hand again and held on to it as she pulled away, but not so hard.

'My chair is me Babe. You hate me.'

'No I don't. You know I don't.' Indignant.

'Yes okay. Not me exactly, but you hate that I can't give you another child.' He paused. 'I do too. I hate me for the same reason. I hate you for the same reason, but I love you more for what we already have. It would be great to have another baby, but whatever happens, all that counts is I love you. I love you Mary.'

Her anger eased a little and the frown lines softened slightly, until Gordon added, 'But not as much as my chair.'

Now she smiled.

'So I choose the chair Babe. I'll help you pack.'

'I'm going nowhere. YOU'RE going, and take your heap of shit with you.' The anger had gone and they were back to normal banter.

'Tell you what Babe. Give me a chance to keep the chair. Scissors, paper, stone?'

'NO,' shouted Mary, angry again.

'Okay, okay,' Gordon back-tracked, knowing he had pushed his luck. 'Okay, I'll compromise. You let me buy a shed and the dentist chair can move out to the garden.'

'Deal.'

Gordon took another sip of Mythos and a mouthful of moussaka.

Mary's line of thought had been identical to Gordon's and she sat with her wine held in front of her face, studying the droplets of condensation on the glass with Nigel in her head, playing on his own in the back yard of 18 Granville Terrace, an only child despite their best efforts. She had blamed Gordon, wrongly, but she couldn't help it, and even now after so many years, she felt a little twinge of guilt. She had even threatened to leave him unless he threw his beloved dentist chair away.

'No. Not really,' repeated Mary.

'What?'

'My twin. Think about it.'

'Oh right.' Gordon finished his beer. 'More wine Babe,' he asked Mary as he caught the waiter's eye and jiggled his empty glass with a smile.

The waiter nodded, returned his smile and disappeared.

Mary reached across the table, took Gordon's hand and looked back at the sun setting on the olive groves. 'It's beautiful here. And there is nobody I would rather share it with than you Gordon.'

'That's nice,' said Gordon bluntly, a little surprised by her sudden intimacy, then thinking he ought to be a little more sincere in his response to avoid rebuke, 'It is.' Not enough. Try harder. 'And yes. Me too. With you I mean.'Oops. Sincerity lost through awkward sentence construction.

'But I still can't wait to get home and see the grand-kids.' Mary smiled and they both turned as a police car pulled up outside the restaurant.

The policeman sauntered across to the waiter for a quiet word. He then pointed across to Mary and Gordon, before heading over.

'Unbelievable officer. Drinks crate on the end of a rope. One bump and the toddler is on the Tarmac.'

The policeman took off his hat. 'Mind if I sit?'

Gordon and Mary looked at each other.

'No. Go ahead,' Gordon gestured towards a free chair with his hand.

The officer said nothing, but sat with his elbows resting on the table and looked at them expectantly in turn, first Mary, then Gordon, then back to Mary. They both looked at him, then back at each other, then back at him.

The music faded out, then the soft groans of injured passengers faded in. The smell of cheap wine and moussaka was replaced by the smell of hot metal and burning oil.

'No,' screamed a man on the other side of the bus a little way back. Then the policeman leant forward, blew out the candle and all was silent.

'Sorry. Time's up. I need your answer now.'

'Can I just ask you one more thing?'

'Go on then.'

'You said we were both on your list three other times. You told us all three for Gordon but only two for me?'

'Ah yes.' The Grim Reaper sat back in his chair. 'Funnily enough, you touched on it over dinner.'

Mary nodded.

'When your mother was pregnant?' Grim added almost as a question, expecting Mary to fill in the gaps.

'Twins?' she replied.

'Yes.'

Mary's lip quivered.

'I had to take one of you,' he shrugged. 'I chose your twin.'

Mary looked back at her wine and again studied the droplets on the glass for a moment.

'But we were unborn babies?'

'A life is a life.' Grim thought that was more than enough explanation .

After another pause. 'Was my twin a girl?'

Grim wondered for a moment if this information could be shared. Don't see why not. 'Yes.'

Mary smiled.

Gordon smiled.

Mary had one more question. 'How did you choose which baby to ... you know?'

Grim looked a little bashful. 'Hmm. Not easy. Not much to go on with babies.'

Mary nodded encouragement.

Grim shrugged again. 'Sorry ... but it was scissors, paper, stone ... with my brother.'

Mary snorted.

Gordon couldn't help a smile. 'Fair enough Mary. We do that often enough.'

They sat in silence. Grim was patient while Gordon and Mary held both hands together over the table and looked into each other's eyes, which welled with tears, Mary first, followed closely by Gordon.

'Let's do it that way Gordon.'

He nodded.

'Just once. None of your best of three rubbish.'

She smiled and they both held up their hands and thumped their fists into their palms.

'One, two, three,' they croaked together.

Gordon had stone. Mary had scissors.

21 ... **Just do it Geoff**

10 minutes after the crash, Wednesday, April 11, 1984: 'All she saw was a silhouette of a gun. Far away on the other side,' sang Maggie

Reilly on Mike Oldfield's Moonlight Shadow. The speakers at the front of the bus had stopped working and the ripple of music from the back of the bus was almost lost in the cacophony of distress. Seconds later, it came to an abrupt end.

'He was shot six times by a man on the run,' sounded normal, but 'And she couldn't find how to push through,' went up an octave and accelerated as the cassette player chewed up the tape.

The fire was tracking along the oil spill outside the bus towards the fuel pipe but there were no flames inside ... just stifling heat.

'Rocks,' shouted John Coyle, still suspended from his two trapped fingers. 'When you get out, bring back rocks and load them on the front.'

His words were almost lost in the panic as passengers struggled towards the gaping front window of the bus.

'Help me friend. Help me,' squealed Spiros Gekas, the driver, reaching out and trying to grab the passengers as they escaped. He struggled but was gripped firmly in his twisted seat against the crushed front corner of the bus.

The passengers flapped at his outstretched arm. Ilias helped them out, but heard John Coyle, the same voice that had warned him when he first tried to smash the windscreen. He grabbed the next passenger by the arm, a teenage boy with a startled sun-burned face.

'What's he saying?' Ilias asked desperately, but the boy knew no Greek and looked as if he were about to burst into tears.

Ilias shook him and pointed to where the sound came from.

John shouted again. 'Get rocks. Everybody. Don't just run. Get rocks.'

'Rocks,' shouted the teenager and pointed to a boulder at the side of the road.

Ilias worked it out and grabbed the rock. With it in his hands he shouted after the fleeing passengers. 'Come back and help. We need rocks.'

In the blind panic, most people didn't hear him, those that did spoke no Greek but a couple of women worked it out and ran back.

John Coyle felt encouraged and started looking around for his tool bag. Geoff was still drifting in and out of consciousness.

John kicked and twisted until he freed his legs but yelped as some of his weight shifted onto his fingers. As his body uncurled his feet found the parcel shelf and he steadied himself. He shuffled through the debris with his foot until he found his canvas tool bag, then hooked his foot through the handle and lifted it to his free hand.

Unzipping the bag with one hand wasn't easy but he got it open enough to squeeze his hand in and pull out his secateurs.

He thought about making the cut himself but knew he would pass out after the first finger and bleed to death while still pinned by the last finger.

'Geoff. Geoff. I need your help.'

'Sorry Kez. I'm so sorry.'

John shook him and scratched the back of his hand with the secateurs blade. He had no idea if this would help but remembered scratching the back of his neck, almost to the point of drawing blood, when he had tried to stop falling asleep after driving for almost six hours through the night many years ago.

'Fuck off Coyle. What d'you do that for?'

Result.

'Listen Geoff. I need your help.' He held the secateurs in front of Geoff's face. 'Take these. You have to cut my fingers off.'

'You must be fucking joking. I can't do that.'

John tried to be firm. 'Geoff. You have to. If you don't, we both die.'

'Help's here. Let's just wait.'

'Fuck it Geoff. There's one man. He's helped get people off the bus and now we're on fire and a bit further off the cliff. We may only have seconds. Cut my fingers off, then wrap this hanky over the stumps to stop the bleeding.'

Geoff's eyes opened wide in alarm. He gingerly took the secateurs.

'Geoff. I will pass out. I know I will. You have to bring me round so I can get you out. My crowbar is in the other tool bag. I can probably free you.'

Geoff looked dazed.

'Mate, if I don't come round, scratch the back of my hand with the secateurs blade.'

Geoff shut his eyes and shook his head.

'Just do it Geoff.'

Geoff wanted to drift off. I don't mind if I die. Nobody would miss me. Costa wouldn't care. Kez wouldn't care. I have only known Coyley a few weeks. Why should he care? If I didn't help him and I die, so be it. Fine. I want to die. It would be a relief. I could help John but he will probably save me if I free him. Do I really want that?

John could see he was losing Geoff.

'Look you selfish bastard. It's not just you. You may want your pathetic life over but

I want to live. I have a family. I can save some of these people. They have families. You might have nothing to live for but they have. Cut my fucking fingers off.'

With that Geoff lunged across John with the secateurs gaping open, pushed them over his two trapped fingers, and squeezed as hard as he could. It didn't take much. He felt the give in the bone as the blades slid through and clicked shut, much the same as cutting through a small branch. John slithered down and Geoff grabbed his arm to break the fall.

He held onto John's arm and wrapped the hanky as tight as he could over the two weeping stumps.

John threw his head back to avoid the sweep of the scythe. He managed to duck his head just in time but his hands went forward to balance the movement and the sharp blade took off two fingers.

John recovered and jumped back. 'Whoa ... you nearly had me then.'

The Grim Reaper stood facing John with blood dripping from his glistening weapon.

'Riding your luck young man, but you're not safe yet.' Grim had been friendly the first time John spoke to him, but his voice had an edge to it now. There was a hint of menace.

213

John felt no fear, firm in the belief that his own fate was out of his hands.

They stood facing each other, neither moving.

After, what seemed like many minutes, but must have been seconds, the Grim Reaper pulled back his black hood, his scythe was now a guitar and he started singing. He was Bob Dylan.

'When you're sad and when you're lonely, And you haven't got a friend, Just remember that death is not the end.'

Why the fuck am I listening to Bob Dylan when I need to be helping people? John interrupted the song.

'Bob.'

'John.'

'Can I go?'

'Just click your fingers mate.' He chuckled at his cruel joke.

'Seriously, I have to go.'

'Fine.' Bob put down his guitar. 'But before you go.'

'What?' John was impatient.

Grim didn't want to be hurried.

'You've got issues man.'

'Like what?'

'Like Giles Thornton, successful property developer. Chairman of YMCA Football Club.'

'And?'

'And you had a head full of drivel when you refereed a cup match. Thought you were being bribed.'

John felt a bit stupid.

'He's genuine. He wouldn't do that. Can't believe you even thought he could. Can't believe you got so low that you toyed with such self-indulgent ideas. The work he subs you on the 200-house site is a generous gift. He could easy do it all. He could easy do the Corfu villa without your help too. He only suggested it to save your pride.'

John felt even more stupid.

'So get over yourself and go save lives.'

The feeling of stupidity fell away and John felt a surge of energy and a scratch on the back of his hand.

Bob walked away and shouted back over his shoulder, 'Nobody is free, even the birds are chained to the sky.'

Geoff scratched the back of John's hand until he broke the skin.

John felt the blood racing through his head. His fingers throbbed, but the chaotic images circling in his brain slowed enough for him to put them in order and focus on where he was. He looked around and winced as a jolt of sharp pain ran up his arm from his severed fingers.

'Alright Coyley? Didn't see that coming did you?' Geoff forced a laugh.

'Good man Geoff. Good man.'

John found his other tool bag and grabbed his crow bar. He could hear the crackle of flames overhead as he tried to lever the seats apart. Sweat dripped from his forehead. The heat from the fire was sapping his strength.

'Arghh,' screamed Geoff. 'Hurts even more when the pressure comes off.

John could move the seat a little but it sprung back onto Geoff's leg when he took away the crowbar and Geoff stayed pinned like a very fat and sweaty butterfly.

Ilias and the red-faced teenager, helped by the two women were still loading rocks on the front end, trying not to block the escape route but the loss of so many passengers left the bus straining on the tow rope. The fire had also reduced the weight of the bus at the front and there was a small judder as the bus ground another couple of inches over the edge and tilted slightly to one side before again coming to a rest.

'I can move a bit,' shouted Geoff.

The bus had tipped sideways for the first time. Spilled oil now trickled towards the fuel pipe and the flames followed close behind.

The twisting of the bus had taken some of the pressure off Geoff's legs.

John rammed the bar back between the seats. 'Right, when I swing on this, give yourself a good push.'

22 ... **That can't be right**

Just after the crash, Wednesday, April 11, 1984: 'Wow. What a big scythe you've got.'

Lucy Birdham felt no pain. So this is it. I'm dead. And here's the Grim Reaper ready to slice my head off. Just like the movies. Didn't expect that. At 28 years old, Lucy felt a bit disappointed. She was a fun-loving free spirit and the thought of dying had never passed through her mind. The death of her cat had been her only experience of grief and she really didn't know how to feel.

She certainly didn't feel pain and, strangely, she felt no fear, even though a heavily cloaked, and hooded, demon stood in front of her with an exceptional weapon, the shining blade almost as long as the handle.

'So. Mr Reaper. Am I dead?'

'Sorry Lucy, but yes.'

She raised her eyebrows with casual acceptance. Although there was a bizarre absence of fear, pain and any of the cliché emotions associated with death, she did have a nagging feeling that she had been given a raw deal. The Reaper had apologised. Maybe he had got the wrong person.

'Are you going to cut my head off?'

'No. No need. You're already dead.'

'Oh right.' She looked along the length of his blade. 'What's the scythe for then?'

'It's a prop.' She looked lost. 'Just so you know who I am.'

She nodded. 'Okay. What now then?'

'I'll walk you over to the collection point and you can have a drink while I finish on the bus.'

'Lovely. Thanks Mr Reaper. What do you still have to do?'

'Just gotta fill my quota.'

Lucy nodded again. 'Oh right. How many today?'

'At least 16.'

Lucy looked around. 'Looks like you're nearly done then.'

Grim stepped forward and took her arm in his and led her off the bus and headed towards the row of white tables with pastel coloured umbrellas.

Lucy stopped and looked back at the bus, a Greek man frozen in the act of throwing a rock in through the front window.

'Oh blimey. It's Ilias. Nice bloke. Was in his bar two days ago.'

She looked back at Grim. The nagging feeling was still there. She held her gaze for a moment.

'Why me?' Then before he could answer. 'I mean, was I just unlucky or what? Or was I being punished? Not that it matters. Looks pretty much a done deal, but did I do wrong?'

He considered her but said nothing.

'Am I a bad person?'

He led her to the table with the peach umbrella and sat her down opposite Mary Teal and Roy Farrell. They exchanged polite greetings before Grim took the spare chair next to Lucy.

Grim waved to Keres and she came over with her notepad.

'Could I have a coffee please Keres?' Then he turned to Lucy. 'Drink?'

'Oh thanks. Beer please Mr Reaper.'

Keres scribbled on her pad and moments later returned with their drinks.

Lucy had been looking at the other three tables in the row. She recognised the four noisy boys at the blue table and smiled. They deserved to be there.

The yellow table had a middle-aged couple. She remembered them with two, or maybe three kids. That was a shame. Next, the two women argued under the lilac umbrella with an angry looking Hispanic man sat opposite who had made her feel uneasy.

She took a sip of her beer and faced Grim, her eyes flicking towards the man on the next table.

'So what's his story?'

Grim checked where she was looking. 'Right. Pedro Raphael. He won't be missed. He killed a man many years ago.'

Lucy grimaced. 'Bloody hell. And I got on a bus with him. Anything could have happened.'

Grim smiled at her irony.

'What about the ugly sisters?'

'Well. Funnily enough, they are sisters. They've done nothing wrong really.' He looked at them with a non-committal expression, then turned back to Lucy. 'But they've not done much right either.'

He saw a hint of worry in her face and added, 'Not that you have to. Nobody's obliged to do good deeds. They're considered a bonus. Truth be told, makes no difference.' Then he qualified himself. 'Very little difference anyway.'

Lucy took another mouthful of beer, looked at the bus, the anxious crowd of survivors and the growing group of fascinated onlookers, some grabbing photographs of the stricken bus.

'So you know all about these people?'

'Yes.'

'And you know all about me?'

'Yes,' Grim said softly, trying not to make her feel judged.

A ripple of excitement ran through Lucy. It was quite appealing. All her secrets exposed. She felt naked.

'So come on then Grim. Surely I wasn't just unlucky?'

Grim knew that she was. She had sat in one of his five pre-selected seats. Could have been anybody. She was just unlucky. Unlike some of the others, she had been selected totally at random.

'Yes you were.'

'Nahh.' She wasn't having it.

'You were. You've done nothing to draw undue attention to yourself.'

'Well Grim, there you go. You didn't say I've done nothing. "Nothing to draw undue attention to yourself," is a little bit different.'

Now she took the opportunity to use a word she had always liked but never had chance to use.

'Grim. You're omnipresent. Or at least I get the impression that you are.' She was warming to him and, despite the unusual circumstances, found herself feeling a little flirtatious. 'So come on, make me feel a little less cheated. What's the worst thing I've ever done? You owe me that. Surely? I need something to pin this death on.'

'Nothing Lucy. Can't help you.'

'Are you saying I'm perfect?'

'Not at all.' Almost indignant.

'Go on then. Give me something.'

Grim tapped his fingers on the table and thought hard.

'Okay. The Stiletto Olympics.'

Lucy thought for a second before a big smile spread across her face. She fondly remembered organising the Stiletto Olympics during Rag Week at college. Students, male and female had taken part in a series of athletics events to raise money for cancer

222

research, the only rule being you had to wear six inch heels.

'What's wrong with that? We raised over £2,000.'

'Bio-chemistry undergraduate Mark Snell broke his ankle.'

Lucy was still smiling. 'He was an idiot, drank six cans of lager before the race. Served him right.'

Grim nodded, almost imperceptibly.

'Besides, there were plenty of doctors.'

Another gentle nod.

'But that's not good enough. I must have done worse.'

Lucy waited patiently while Grim thought hard.

He raised his hand and opened his mouth to speak, but changed his mind.

'Go on. What?' Lucy insisted.

'Nothing.'

'Something,' urged Lucy. 'You thought of something. Come on. Tell me.'

Grim placed both hands on the table and took a deep breath.

'Right. Got to make this clear. I can remember one thing you did, but it had absolutely nothing to do with today's bus crash. You were picked at random today. Just plain unlucky, but if it helps, you can blame this.'

Lucy smiled expectantly.

'You were an A-level student.'

'Okay.'

'1974. You were a member of the Students Against Vietnam Society.'

'I remember.'

'And you took part in a publicity stunt against your MP.'

'Arhh.' Lucy's smile faded a little. 'That was a bit naughty.'

'Yes. So naughty, you never claimed it. Not going to stop a war if nobody knew you did it.'

'True. Went too far though.'

Lucy and her 'comrades' had released a bright orange six-foot Corn Snake from a property one field away from their MP's house in the hope that it would cross the field and scare the 'war mongering' politician.

Unfortunately, the snake's natural instinct was to avoid the open spaces and head for the cover of the woods behind the snake house, which were bounded by a primary school. The kids were learning about farming and had been keeping chickens. There was plenty of food for the snake and lots of cover.

Nobody had been hurt but a lot of kids had been mentally scarred with an unreasonable fear of snakes. The Students Against Vietnam Society had kept a low profile.

'Nobody got hurt,' Lucy defended herself.

'Yeah. I know. Like I said. No harm done, but that's the best I can offer you.'

As he spoke, Grim looked past Lucy at the bus.

All was still, the flames didn't move, the smoke went nowhere, there was no sound and all the people were frozen like a still from a film, but Grim noticed movement in one of the windows.

He stood up. 'Sorry Lucy. Won't be a minute.' He walked towards the bus.

There was a man waving.

Nobody moves. This is my show. I run this party.

As he got closer, he could clearly see a bearded man, possibly in his sixties, but he had a look that could be much younger or older. He was looking straight at Grim. He was waving at the Grim Reaper and beckoning him over. He had started waving while Grim was sat at the four tables of the collection point. Nobody on the bus could see those tables. Something was not as it should be and, for once, Grim was unsettled, out of his comfort zone.

He walked up to the bus and knelt down in front of the window, tilting his head a little, bemused.

The man smiled and waved him closer.

23 ... **The bearded man**

10 minutes after the crash, Wednesday, April 11, 1984: It felt like a flea. The Grim Reaper scratched his ear with his back paw.

He sat on the lap of the bearded man.

Now this is a first. I've never been a cat before.

Grim welcomed the strange twist of events with mild amusement and what, in feline terms, passed as a smile, but that immediately turned to horror as he heard a man further down the bus shout, 'Just do it Geoff,' and he felt the searing heat of the fire on the top of the wreck.

Why was he on the bus in real time? He tried to run for the open window at the front but was restrained by the bearded man. He had a thousand questions but no voice.

Suddenly he was sharing the nightmare with his victims. It was an alien feeling. He was used to having total control. He was the puppet master. He had studied all 49 passengers before the crash. He knew them all intimately but this man was a stranger. He didn't know his name, age, nationality, background, likes, dislikes and he certainly didn't know anything about the highs and lows of his life.

And more than that. He appeared to have no conscious thoughts. Everybody else's thoughts were broadcast like a blaring radio but a calm silence radiated from this man.

Smiling through his beard, the man gazed at Grim with intense warmth, reassuring warmth, the same reassuring warmth that Grim had cultivated.

'No need to struggle.' His voice was as smooth as a cooing dove and his words melted into Grim's fur like the comfort blanket of a bedtime story.

'While you are with me, the bus will not fall. There will be no explosion. The flames will stay outside the bus.'

He spoke slowly and Grim relaxed a little, although instinct told him to keep one eye on his escape route.

His smile was fixed and he rubbed Grim behind the ears, stroked his fur and looked around the bus. 'Nice job. You've got the referee building himself up for heroic deeds, the fat decorator wallowing in self pity.' He nodded approval of Grim's handiwork.

'And I like what you did with the two elderly couples. Scissors, paper, stone. Nice touch.'

Although a shade more relaxed physically, Grim's emotions were in a whirlpool of confusion. Who was this man? Why was he here? How did he know all these things?

It was a long time since Grim had been so far outside his comfort zone. His mind flashed back to his very first job.

'Now then, youngster. Remember. A lot of people die every day. You can't be there for every death. So there's little margin for error. Get in there. Do the job. Get out.'

Grim had smiled with a confidence that disappeared as soon as the gravity of the job hit him.

'We have a lorry crash here. Brakes fail, it ploughs straight through red lights at a busy crossroads, turns sharply to avoid a queue of cars, rolls and slides on its side into a petrol station, finishing with a crunching smash into three fuel pumps.'

Grim nodded.

'There are 163 people in the immediate vicinity of the crash. One must die. Just one, but you can go over the quota. That's fine.'

Grim had spent what seemed like forever talking with all 163 people, but after hearing their tales of woe and pleas for lenience, had allowed the tipping truck to narrowly miss the entire queue of traffic before sliding over an empty pavement, which had been full of pedestrians only seconds earlier, then letting the truck hit the three fuel pumps at the only time they were all empty during a particularly busy shift.

There had been no explosion and it was only as the driver and his passenger were pulled unhurt from the wreck of the truck that he realised he hadn't even filled his quota of one.

He reluctantly gave the elderly garage owner a heart attack as he stood behind the counter watching the drama unfold.

'Alright Coyley? Didn't see that coming did you?'

Geoff Miller's voice dragged Grim back from the petrol station and he instinctively jumped for the exit but was restrained again, gently but firmly.

Grim realised he had been so absorbed by the stranger that he had noticed nothing of him beyond the beard, his captivating smile and his almost hypnotic eyes.

There was a faint tattoo on the back of his hand, which looked liked a star. Grim looked closer as the man's hand ran along his fur. It was the Star of David.

Quickly Grim looked for his other hand, but it was around his neck. There was another tattoo. Too close to focus.

His beard was bushy and wild but his head was shaved. He wore a long orange cape.

The man swapped hands and Grim saw the second tattoo was the star and crescent.

A Jewish tattoo on one hand with a Muslim tattoo on the other. Strange. Grim wanted to ask him what they meant.

But the burning question which gnawed at Grim with as much persistence as the flea behind his ear was why are you here?

'I want say goodbye and complete your quota.' The man answered as if Grim's thought had been spoken.

Before Grim could splutter out a flood of questions in the hope that this man knew exactly what he was thinking, he lifted his hand off Grim's fur and held it up in a gesture that clearly said, 'Quiet now. Just listen.'

'You have worked well today. The couple in seats seven and eight will take you up to 15 souls. Obviously they are next on your list.'

Grim purred.

'I am coming with you. You don't need to know who I am. Just think of me as number 16.'

Grim felt the bus judder and heard the flames crackle above him.

'I am staying here for now, but I will take the final seat at the lilac table next to Pedro.'

The man held Grim up to his face and held his flank against his cheek, with great affection.

'Like I said, you have done good work. You always do good work. You have become a fine reaper. Now go. We can talk again later.'

The man put Grim down and stroked him gently with both hands.

'But don't forget.'

The bearded man nodded towards Gordon Teal.

'Love of two is one. Here but now they're gone. Don't fear the reaper.'

Grim jumped along the bus and out through the broken windscreen. He stopped at a safe distance to look back at the bearded man, who was unhurt, unruffled and not trapped in any way. He made himself comfortable, leaned back and closed his eyes like he was going to sleep after a long and hard, but rewarding days work.

24 ... **Navia aut caput**

11 minutes after the crash, Wednesday, April 11, 1984: 'Thana. What's up?'

Thanatos stood facing the bus with his arms folded. He was flustered. His focus was gone and he didn't hear Hypnos.

'Thanatos.' He raised his voice.

Grim turned towards his brother to answer but before he could, there was a grinding sound from the bus as it edged a couple more inches over the cliff.

'Nearly went then,' Hypnos sounded anxious. He had never seen his brother's concentration broken. 'Look mate. I know it's not a sheer drop, but there's only so many times the bus can slip further over the edge and still find a sticking point. It's a very steep slope. It's gonna go.'

'Think your right.'

They both stared at the bus. The rope was taut, the olive tree was bent almost to the ground like a cartoon tree waiting to propel Wile E Coyote to distant hills after a failed attempt to stop the Road Runner.

'I didn't think it would, but now I'm not sure.'

'You got much left to do?'

'Not much. Better get busy.'

John Coyle heaved on the bar until he felt the blood vessels in his face almost burst. He felt as if he would rip his own muscles if he pushed any harder and still Geoff stayed rigid in the compressed gap between the seats.

John lost his footing and cursed as the whole bus juddered another couple of inches over the edge.

The bar fell at the feet of five-year-old Sally Whisper. She picked it up and held it out towards the sweaty man with a blood-soaked hanky on his hand.

As John took it, he made a quick mental calculation before turning back to Geoff.

'Sorry mate. I'm going to have to come back for you.'

He grabbed the little girl's hand and started to lead her to the front of the bus.

'No,' she shouted, pulling on his arm.

'What?'

'That man said to keep still.' She pointed at an elderly man who was cradling his wife in his arms. 'And I have to wait for my family.'

John picked up the younger boy, carried him under his arm, dragged the girl and told the older boy to follow.

'Our parents and grand-parents need help,' pleaded the older boy.

'I WILL come back for them. I promise.'

The boy looked back through his tears, not sure what to do, but followed the sweaty man.

John helped them through the windscreen.

'Join the others over there and stay well clear.' He gave them a stern look. 'You hear me. Stay well clear.'

They nodded and scurried away in a close huddle as John worked his way past the growing pile of rocks in the bus towards the back.

This could go any second. There's too many people. I need more time.

His mind was racing. He looked frantically around, all the time prioritising the passengers. There were a lot of dead bodies and a lot of trapped people. I need more time.

Suddenly a plan fell into place. Gotta move dead bodies forward, use their weight.

He picked out a Hispanic man's body. He had a pock-marked face. John was pretty certain he was dead, but even more certain that if he was wrong, the man would let him know.

Pain shot up his arm from his bleeding hand as he tugged on the man's collar and slowly edged him up the bus. His adrenalin was acting as a painkiller but the agony was still intense. He was light headed with loss of blood and the extreme heat. But he ignored it, dumped the pock-marked man and went back.

After struggling with two plump women in their fifties, he had another brainwave and tentatively looked out through the side door, beyond the cliff edge, and along the outside of the bus.

If I can take off the petrol cap, the tank will empty. The bus is upside down so it will all pour straight down the cliff. Better be quick though before the flames get any closer.

He hooked his injured arm around the rail by the door and leant out as far as he could. He couldn't quite reach the filler cap. Adjusting his position on the rail gave him a little more reach and he struggled with the cap until it fell on the rocks and bounced swiftly down the slope, followed by a steady flow of fuel, much of it soaking John's arm.

He jumped back on the bus, wiped his arm and gingerly made his way towards the back of the bus, where he found two more bodies, a middle-aged couple. The woman looked very much like the little girl he had just helped off. The next two seats were empty and below them an elderly couple lay twisted on top of each other.

John tried to go past them, again thinking they were dead, but the woman's arm twitched. He untangled them and grabbed the woman round the waist. She was an easy lift after the dead weight of the two bigger women. He placed her just outside the front window.

'Please. Come and help,' he shouted over to the crowd.

Two young men ran over as John headed back down the bus for the man, probably her husband, who was now sitting up. John tried to lift him.

He screamed. 'No.'

John looked him up and down. His left leg was bent at an unnatural angle. Must be broken. I will cause more damage if I move him, but time is short. John grabbed him around the waist and lifted him over his shoulder.

The old man shrieked with pain before passing out as John lowered him gently outside the front window.

A Greek man took him from there.

'Please help me,' shouted the driver, trapped upside down in his seat. He was trying to grab John, but couldn't reach.

'I will. Not yet though.'

There were a lot of trapped people and John's crowbar was not up to the job. He saw the parked van, ran over and threw open the back doors.

Geoff Miller sat in front of his black and white telly in a big armchair. He had a beer in one hand and a betting slip in the other with the Soviet Union written on it. It was 1968 and he was watching Italy play the Soviet Union in the semi-final of the European Championships.

It was 0-0 at full time and 68,582 football fans, crowded into the Naples stadium, watched as extra time failed to separate the two teams.

'Shit,' bellowed Geoff as Kurt Tschenscher blew the final whistle.

He was on the edge of his seat. The beer can was empty. He crunched it and threw it in the corner, where it bounced on the rim of the bin and fell to the floor with the other three empty cans that had also failed to hit the target.

He studied his betting slip.

'What happens now?'

Geoff had a week's wages on the Soviet Union to win the whole tournament. He couldn't afford to make the bet, but he needed the money and why not? The Soviet Union played good football. Easy money.

His mouth dropped open in horror.

What the fuck?

The referee showed the Soviet captain a coin. He called it and Kurt tossed the coin in the air. The whole of Europe watched as the coin twisted up and fell to the ground.

The Soviet captain bowed forward with his hands over his mouth.

The Italian skipper's face lit up and both arms shot in the air. His team mates all rushed forward cheering loudly.

Italy had made the final on the toss of a coin.

Geoff had lost a week's wages.

On the toss of a coin.

'Navia aut caput,' said Kes Miller, stood in the doorway behind Geoff.

He turned and saw her face. Disappointed. As always. She hated his gambling but had stuck by him longer than he deserved. She walked into the room, past his chair and over to the telly, which was now colour and twice the size. It was 1978, the year she finally filed for divorce.

She turned the telly off.

'Navia aut caput,' she repeated

'Sorry darling.' He shook his head.

'Ship or head Geoff? It's what the Romans called heads or tails. Gambling was going on long before Geoff Miller first walked in a betting shop.'

He raised his eyebrows.

'Their coins had a ship on one side and the emperor's head on the other.'

He assumed she was making reference to the football match. But she needed to know if he wanted Grim's gamble ... the promise of complete recovery on the toss of a coin, but death if he calls wrong or don't toss a coin and live in a wheelchair for the rest of his life.

'Sorry Kez. Week's wages gone.'

She sighed.

'I'll make it up to you. No more gambling. I promise.'

She laughed.

'And pigs will fly out of my arse.'

Now Geoff laughed.

'Okay Geoff. No more gambling. I believe you.'

She tried not to sound sarcastic. It wasn't easy.

'Anyway Geoff. What's it going to be? Heads or tails?'

He looked confused.

'Or will you finally honour your promise and walk away from a bet.' She paused. 'As you have promised me, time after time, year after year?'

Still confused, Geoff looked around the room. It was no longer 1978. It was 1984. The telly was a suitcase. The pile of empty cans in the corner was a pile of rocks by the front window and his armchair was a bus chair which had been shunted into the seat in front with such force that his legs had been crushed.

'So. The Grim ex-wife. Didn't think I'd ever see you again.'

She shook her head.

'I really am sorry,' it had been habit to apologise to her every time they spoke.

She screwed up her face. 'I know you love me. And I've never stopped loving you. But I always came second to the bookies.'

They were silent. Kez couldn't understand his addiction. Nor could Geoff because Kez was the best thing that ever happened to him and he had slowly driven her away. It was crazy. He knew it was crazy and he still did it.

Kez flipped the coin a few times and waited.

Geoff watched the coin fly through the air and land on the back of her beautiful hand.

He wanted to do the right thing for Kez and refuse the Grim Reaper's bet. He would live. He would be crippled. In a wheelchair for the rest of his life, but alive. It's the safe choice. I'd have to be mad to risk death on the toss of a coin. Then again I'm no use to Kez in a wheelchair. She's probably better off if I die. The only good outcome is winning the toss and getting out of here in one piece.

She stopped tossing the coin and looked deep into his eyes. She had a fair idea what was going through his head.

'Geoff.'

'Kez.'

'You've heard of Sigmund Freud haven't you?'

'No.'

'Yes you have. Famous psychologist, reckons blokes think about sex every minute of the day.'

'Ah yeah. Rings a bell.'

Geoff immediately thought about Kez the first night they had sex in his grubby bedsit, but fought against it and focussed on the bus crash.

'Right. Well he has a theory. You should toss a coin to help make a difficult decision.'

'What? That's it? That's not very deep.'

'Are you goin' to let me finish?'

Geoff nodded for her to carry on.

'He said you shouldn't blindly accept the outcome of the coin toss, but use it to confirm your genuine feelings. You can then ask yourself, "how do I feel about that result?"'

So Kez was suggesting he toss a coin to decide whether he should toss a coin. This was new. Kez was talking him into taking a gamble. Wasn't she? Hard to say no.

'Go on then. Let's try that.'

'Okay. Navia aut caput?

'In English please?'

She rolled her eyes. 'Heads or tails Geoff?'

'And this is just to try the Freud thing?'

'Yes.'

He smiled like a naughty schoolboy.

'Heads and I'll do the toss for real.'

Kez steadied herself, up went the coin, down it came and she slapped her hand over it. She held both hands out to Geoff and slid the top hand away.

'Heads Kez. It's telling me to take the gamble.' He nodded in triumph as if he had won something by calling correctly.

'So? How does it feel?'

He nodded some more.

'Feels good.'

'Why? Cos you actually called it right for once or because you feel good about taking Grim's gamble?'

He looked into the distance, thought about it and then came to a decision.

'Both Kez,' he said with certainty. 'Yes I liked it cause I won. But I want to take the gamble. End of the day. You're not Kez. She's already left me. You're the Grim Reaper. My life's shit already, with good legs. Way I see it. I've got nothing to lose.'

Kez looked alarmed

Geoff was in high spirits. He didn't mind if he lost. The buzz of such a high-stakes gamble was too tempting to refuse.

'Heads Grim.'

Kez tossed the coin again. Geoff followed its flight. She covered it on the back of her hand and held it out to him.

She uncovered the coin.

'Fuck yes,' he shouted with venom through gritted teeth and punched the air. 'Who says I'm unlucky?'

John Coyle grabbed a four-foot length of scaffold pole out of the parked van and ran back to the bus. He crawled along to where Geoff hung unconscious and thrust the pole between the seats. He heaved on it. Geoff fell and landed with a thud. He was heavier than either of the large women but John struggled to the front window with him and the Greek man helped drag him to safety.

25 ... **Bogof**

16 minutes after the crash, Wednesday, April 11, 1984: 'The fire's goin' out Thana.' Keres stood next to her brother watching the drama from a safe distance.

'Yes, but it still might reach the fuel pipe, and the tank.'

'What then?'

'Bang.'

'Is that good or bad?'

Thanatos rubbed his chin. 'Could be good ... or bad.'

Keres looked at him waiting for more.

'Depends. It may tie up a few loose ends or I may overshoot my quota.'

'Would that matter?'

'What? Loose ends or quota?'

'Quota.'

'Yes. Professional pride. I like to deliver on target.'

Keres nodded. 'Fair enough.'

Thanatos pondered his next move. The bearded man was still on his mind, but he pushed those thoughts to one side. He wanted to hit his target and he had two more passengers to take care of. Harry and Megan Zeng were sat in seats seven and eight; the last two of the five seats he had chosen at random before the passengers got on the bus.

'Seats seven and eight then.'

Keres watched him for a moment. 'What you waitin' for Bro?'

Grim sighed. 'Harry Zeng will be hard work. Never takes no for an answer.'

'So? No match for you. Surely?'

'No. S'pose not, but still.'

'Still what?'

'Well. He's your typical cheeky chappy Cockney salesman, hard-working, self-made wealthy man. Chinese father, English mother. Wheeler dealer. Always got an answer.'

'But so have you. And he's one of your 16.'

'Yes, but he's not dead yet. Or his wife. Both trapped ... upside down.'

'You're creative. Think of something.'

'Easy enough for him. He's overweight. All the blood running to his head knocked him out so he's already in trouble. But she's unhurt. Just trapped.'

'Well then, unless you've got anything better, you'll have to make sure the fire reaches the petrol or the bus goes over the edge.'

Thanatos rubbed his chin a little more and sighed again.

A few seconds passed before Keres tried her luck.

'Tell you what. Leave 'em to me.'

Thanatos frowned and sucked in air, almost whistling. 'What? Send in the God of Violent Death to Bargain-Bucket Harry and his doting wife Megan, whose worst act of violence was to shout at a cat for burying its crap in her prize-winning rose garden?'

'Yes. Why not? I've spent most of the day serving drinks and ...' She couldn't think of an 'and'.

Thanatos considered everything he knew about the Zengs. They were the model couple, married 15 years, no kids, wanted them but it never happened, hard-working. Harry had bent the rules now and then and cut a few corners to stay ahead of the game. He had done so quickly and without any sign of remorse and Thanatos wondered just how far he may have stooped if things had not gone smoothly.

'Okay. They're all yours Keres.'

'Don't care what it is Harry, I want lot number seven. It's my lucky number and it's a charity auction. It's a good cause and we're going home tomorrow.'

'Fine Megan. If you want it, it's yours,' Harry hoped it wasn't anything too valuable and he only said yes because he intended buying lot number eight ... whatever it was. That was his lucky number. It never failed him. All his life it had been like a guardian angel. He had met Megan on the eighth of the eighth, 16 years ago. They had got married on the eighth of August the following year. He made his first million eight years after registering as a limited company.

Cheques arrived in the post on the eighth of the month, sometimes from people he thought he would have to chase for months. He had placed his total faith in the number eight and it had never let him down.

Half an hour later, the auctioneer held up lot seven, a broken cigarette lighter. He spoke for a couple of minutes and then took a bid from the front row of 3,000 drachmas.

By the time Harry and Megan had got a translation telling them it was a lighter thought to belong to a German soldier during the 1944 occupation of the island, the bidding had reached 8,000 drachmas.

Megan raised her hand, which Harry immediately pulled down.

'You must be joking. It's broken. You don't smoke and I could get you a lighter for less than a quid anywhere.'

Her face went red and contorted with anger. 'It's lot seven. It's for cancer. Doesn't matter what it is and you said you'd get it.'

Up went her hand again, time after time, until the hammer fell at a price equivalent to £75.

Harry winced.

Megan smiled triumphantly.

The auctioneer held up lot eight - a strange looking knife.

The bidding was higher than the selling price of the lighter before they found out it was a bayonet from the rifle of an Italian soldier who had been killed by the Corfiot resistance in 1942.

At a price which translated to £220, the hammer fell and Harry found himself almost regretting, for the first time, his faith in the number eight.

After 27 more lots, the auctioneer invited the successful bidders to conclude business in a side room.

Harry and Megan were surprised to discover the room was empty apart from an attractive young lady, who was seated at a table. There were two free chairs and she ushered them forward.

They sat quietly and waited.

The young lady finished her paperwork, leant back with arms folded and looked at them.

The room was quiet. And so very empty. Harry felt uncomfortable but waited for the girl to speak.

'There's no such thing as luck,' she said firmly, almost a challenge.

Harry looked at Megan. Who is this woman speaking to us in perfect English and where's my bayonet?

'No such thing,' the woman repeated.

Harry didn't know what was going on. This was a strange room and this was a strange woman.

'Where's our stuff ... lots seven and eight ... German lighter, Italian bayonet?'

As Harry spoke, her cold stare remained unchanged and she did not reply for some time.

'In your yellow bag. The one you always use for hand luggage.'

Again Harry looked at Megan, confused.

He shook his head. 'But you haven't given us them yet.'

'They're in your hand luggage.'

Harry was starting to feel angry.

'Right young lady, listen to me, I have the money for our lots.' He held out his wallet. 'Let's finish the deal and we can go.'

She very slowly shook her head.

'They're in your hand luggage and you're not going anywhere until I've finished with you.'

Harry was used to getting his own way. He stood up abruptly, almost knocking his chair over and reached for Megan's arm. 'Come on Megs, we're not having this. Let's find the auctioneer.'

He marched for the door, pushed hard, it flew open and he almost stepped out, but recoiled in horror. There was a 300 foot drop outside the door to the rocks in the bay above Palaiokastritsa.

'What the fuck,' he exclaimed softly under his breath. He stared uncomprehending at the waves below lapping gently against the shore.

'Please take a seat Mr Zeng,' Keres said, adding, 'Mrs Zeng.'

Harry's confidence melted away. His bravado evaporated and after controlling his rapid breathing and trembling body, he turned, still holding Megan's hand and shuffled slowly back. They both sat down.

He looked down at the table, but saw nothing. He struggled to focus. His mind was a jumble. After a minute, his trance was broken by his wife's quiet sobs. She held him around the waist and wept softly, pressing her face into his chest.

Keres waited patiently and after a couple of minutes, Harry looked up.

'Who are you?' he asked. The anger gone.

'The Grim Reaper.'

Harry looked around the empty room, placed one arm around Megan and stroked her back with what he hoped felt like reassurance.

'Has the auction house blown up or something?'

Keres shook her head. 'No. The auction was yesterday. You're on the airport bus. Crashed . On fire. Balanced on the edge of a cliff, held in place by a short rope fixed to a tree.'

Megan's sobbing increased.

'Oh. And you're upside down trapped in your seats.'

'Dead then?'

'Well. No, actually. You're unhurt, but unconscious. Megan isn't hurt at all, and is fully conscious but you are blocking her escape route.'

Harry's face lit up with fresh hope.

'Will we be rescued?'

'No you'll die.' Keres kept her face straight but inwardly she had to admit enjoying that line.

Harry was starting to get his head around the situation and was now thinking fast. He had made good money thinking fast and cutting deals. 'If we're not dead yet, let's do a deal.'

'No deal,' Keres said, almost cutting him off.

'Hold on. There's always a deal.'

Keres shook her head with disgust. Thanatos had warned her.

'I've made a pretty good living selling all kinds of shit. Stuff people didn't think they wanted. You can sell anything if you put the right price on it. Package it right. People can't help themselves. They say they have no money, but as soon as they sniff a bargain, out comes the wallet.'

He paused hoping to learn something from the Grim Reaper's body language, but she gave nothing away.

'So. What are we looking at here? I have money. You have the power to give or take life. Two lives in our case. How much? Shall I start at one million pounds?'

Keres laughed.

'You really are serious aren't you?'

'Yes,' Harry replied with renewed belief. 'What do you say?'

'I say nothing. I just laugh.'

Undeterred, Harry upped the ante. 'Okay. Fair enough. You play hard ball. Let's make it two million.'

Keres smiled, trying not to look patronising. 'I have no use for money. I deal in life and death. Nothing else. There is no amount of money that will change the fact that when your time is up, your time is up, and you, Mr Zeng, along with your wife, have run out of time. You're coming with me.'

Harry had anticipated resistance but was still confident he could make a deal. 'I hear you,' he nodded. 'I hear you. You don't want money. We can still do business though.' He eased Megan back into her own seat, stood up and started pacing back and forth as he mentally calculated his options.

He stopped and leant forward with one hand on the table.

'Fair enough. I have money, but you don't want it. Thing is though. Plenty of other people do.'

Keres raised her eyebrows in disbelief. 'Yes. But there's nobody else here.'

'I appreciate that. This is between you and me. You deal in life and death. I deal in pounds and pence.'

Harry waited in the hope that the drama would add value to his offer.

'Bogof Grim Reaper.'

Keres couldn't help laughing out loud.

Harry waited again. 'Buy one, get one free. Works every time. Whenever I have stock that I've got to move, I do a bogof promotion. It even works if you put up the price of one. As soon as people think they're getting something free, they can't resist.'

'And?'

'And that's what I'm offering you.'

'But I'm not buying.'

'Depends how you look at it.'

Keres didn't follow.

'Me and Megan. Two lives.' Harry nodded as if responding to himself. 'Let us live and I'll deliver you four other lives.'

Keres was dumfounded. This was new.

'What? You offering to kill four people for me?'

'If that's what it takes.'

'How easy do you think it is to murder somebody?'

'Like I said, I have money. I'd hire someone to do it for me.'

'No good.'

'Why not?'

Keres knew a life was a life according to the rules, but Harry didn't need to know that.

'Against the rules. No murders. Has to be natural causes,' she lied.

'I'll pay four terminally ill people to kill themselves. Their families would never want for anything.'

Keres was starting to see why Thanatos had been reluctant to deal with Harry, but she didn't have her brother's weakness. Thanatos liked neat tidy jobs. He was a perfectionist.

He would persist with a debate until he won. She was the God of Violent death and the discussion was over.

'Harry. No deal. You and Megan die.'

John Coyle was dripping with sweat. He was still losing blood, but not so fast. The congealed mass of blackened blood on the hanky was slowing the flow, but every time he used what remained of his hand, another pulse oozed out. Moving Geoff had been hard work, but now he looked up at an even larger man, wedged upside down in seat number eight.

He pushed the scaffold pole in between the seats and swung on it. The woman in seat seven was much smaller than the man and she fell first. She was unhurt and grabbed her yellow hand luggage and sat with her back against the window and her bag on her legs.

John took a breather before swinging on the bar again. Something in the back of the seat snapped and the man fell straight down, head first onto the bag on his wife's legs.

The woman screamed. It was a deafening sound and she didn't stop. The man didn't move. John put the bar down and leaned across for a better look. He couldn't help a small scream of his own as he saw the point of what looked like an old bayonet sticking out of the man's mouth. It must have been in the bag on the woman's lap and appeared to have impaled him through the back of his neck. His wife, having been free for a few seconds was now trapped under his dead body.

26 ... **I need my locket**

18 minutes after the crash, Wednesday, April 11, 1984: Megan Zeng was breathing faster and faster in between hysterical screams.

John Coyle tried to lift Harry's body off her, but it had wedged itself between two twisted sheets of roofing material and the parcel shelf.

Megan was hyperventilating and John could do nothing.

He prodded the scaffold pole between Harry's back and the parcel shelf, but as he levered, the pole tore into the dead man's flesh.

John tried to think, but he was feeling light-headed from the heat, exhaustion and loss of blood. His head was ringing and all he could hear was the driver shouting.

He was close to panic, too many people needed help, time was short and nobody else had dared venture onto the bus to help for fear it may fall.

Fuck me. What am I doing? I have to get off this bus. I don't want to die.

He started picturing Sarah at home with Peter and Chloe arguing over Monopoly. Trivial thoughts started running through his head.

I have to get home. My parents' golden wedding party is at my house this weekend. Gotta get ready for it. Marquee needs putting up. Grass needs cutting. Hedge strimming.

Just before he slipped into unconsciousness, he felt a man shaking him by the shoulder and quickly focussed.

'Please. Please help me.'

The man looked about ten years older than John, but very weak. He struggled like a much older man. He had clearly been hurt but there were no visible injuries. John grabbed his arm to lead him to the front.

'No. No.' He yanked his arm free. 'My wife is having an asthma attack I have to find her inhaler.'

John had a fresh surge of adrenalin and was again thinking fast.

'Where is she?'

The man led him to the woman who looked startled as she hunted for air, wedged between a heavy suitcase and a large bald man with a big bushy beard and long orange cloak.

John grabbed the woman's husband by the shoulders and looked him in the eye.

'Listen. We have to get her off the bus. That's her best chance.'

The man wasn't convinced. His eyes flitted around still looking for the bag with the inhaler.

'There will be help on the way and the best thing for an asthma attack is clear air. It could be the fumes in here causing the attack. Now help me get her off.'

John grabbed her and draped her over his shoulder before picking his way through the debris and handing her to other helpers waiting at the front window.

As the fresh air hit her, she inhaled and whispered for her husband. 'Roy.'

He put his ear to her mouth.

'My locket.'

She struggled again but had enough strength to grab him fiercely by the hair and yank him towards her mouth.

'Get my locket.'

She struggled for breath and Roy broke away from her grip.

'Where is it?' he shouted desperately, wanting more than anything to do whatever would bring a smile back to her face.

She tried to speak but couldn't.

'Is it with your inhaler?'

She stopped flapping her hands and nodded.

Roy was back in the bus before John could stop him.

John raced after him but gave up the pursuit as an elderly woman reached out for him. He stopped and his eyes danced over the woman and her friend taking in all the detail. They were both alive but their seats had come away from the floor and pushed them up against the window. The gap was too narrow for them to squeeze out.

John looked around for his scaffold pole and poked it through the gap, past the women and smashed it through the window. The large window spanned three pairs of seats and once he had broken most of it away, there was space for the women to get out.

The woman reached back through the gap and held John's arm. 'Thank-you.' Then they were out through the window and the Greek man helped them away to safety.

John looked around and saw an elderly man near the side door towards the back of the bus cradling a woman in his arms. As he edged towards him, the bus creaked. He started throwing bags and anything he could lay his hands on up the bus before edging further towards the back.

'Please. Help my wife.'

John looked at her. There was no movement. He tried for a pulse and gently shook his head.

'I'm sorry. She's gone.'

The man sobbed and hugged her tight. 'Mary. Mary.' He kissed her and rocked her gently in his arms.

John could see it would be hard getting the man off the bus. He placed his good hand on the man's shoulder.

'You've got to get off mate. This bus is going over the cliff.'

The man appeared not to hear and carried on rocking Mary gently in his arms.

John tried again but the old man kept sobbing 'no'. John was on the verge of forcing him off the bus when the creaking noise grew louder with Roy heading further towards the back in search of his wife's locket.

Then John heard a loud crack and felt the bus tip sharply.

Ilias Vyntra had been tempted to get on the bus and help the tourist with the bloody hand, but he could see how far over the tree was being pulled by his rope tethered to the front bumper of the bus and decided it was too much of a gamble. He got as close as he could to help passengers away as they came to the front window.

After carrying a wheezing woman away from the wreck and leaving her with other survivors for medical help, Ilias ran back to the front window. He studied the driver's situation and was about to take a calculated risk by stepping inside the window to try and free him when he heard glass breaking along the clear side of the bus.

He ran round and saw the end of his scaffold pole thrusting out through the window.

His brother George had persuaded him to carry a heavy hydraulic jack in his van, but it had been his own idea to carry the scaffold pole. An idea he was now quite proud of.

Without getting too close, Ilias could see two women just inside the window and when the blood-soaked tourist finished knocking out the glass he helped the women out. He carried the first back round the front of the bus, stooped under the rope and away to safety before going back for the other.

He cradled the second woman in his arms like a baby and headed back for safety and, stooping under the rope, he heard the high pitched noise of splitting wood, followed by a loud crack as a branch came free.

The branch had been stopping the rope sliding along the now-horizontal tree trunk towards the bus, which began tipping further over the cliff.

The rope abruptly snagged on another branch but started to slip around the trunk. The bus tipped more. The far end of the rope was tied to the van and as the loops of rope wrapped round the tree slid, the van started to take the strain of the bus.

Ilias watched, mouth wide open, as his van slid slowly towards the tree and the bus tipped still further. The front of the bus was ten feet off the ground before the van slid up against the tree and came to rest once more. There were no verbal thoughts passing through his mind, just a jumble of horrific images. The blood-soaked rescuer plummeting to his death in an explosive crunch of metal, the driver's cries for help finally falling silent, and, with a touch of guilty embarrassment, a shiny new van purchased with the insurance money.

John felt like he left his stomach ten feet above where he now stood as the back of the bus dropped for what seemed like an eternity. He started to face the inevitable. It was just as he had often heard. His life raced before his eyes, obviously not all of it, but the highlights, much the same as here's-your-best-bits when a contestant leaves a reality television show.

When the bus came to a standstill, all he could think about was Sarah and the kids. He wanted to tell them how much he loved them. Not when he got home, but now. He wanted to tell them right now. And hug them.

He looked down at the old man, now pressed up against the broken seats as the bus tilted at an awkward angle. He could see his whole body shaking with fear. He turned away and wretched, repeatedly.

Come on John. Get a grip. You're not dead yet. Get the old man out while you still can.

He grabbed his shoulder firmly.

'Look mate. We have to get off the bus. Now.'

Many of the rocks that had been piled up at the front of the bus had fallen towards the back when the bus tipped and it was tough finding a way through the mess.

The old man was still reluctant, even though he had come close to death and he looked back at Mary as John struggled with him up the steeply canted bus and out through the smashed side window, which was only a couple of feet above the road-side verge.

27 ... **Plan B**

22 minutes after the crash, Wednesday, April 11, 1984: The hairs on the back of John Coyle's neck stood on end as creaks and groans echoed through the corpse of the bus, which now reeked of death.

After a mental stock take, John made a quick decision.

The idiot looking for his locket. He can get off himself so I'm not helping him until last. The woman squashed under her husband. She could take a while. The driver. Need more time.

Now the grieving old man had gone, he grabbed his wife and dragged her up the bus to the front.

He could still hear the 'idiot' rifling through the debris for his wife's hand luggage. Not even worth arguing with him.

Then he went for the bald man with the beard and grabbed him by his feet, but dropped him instantly as the man's eyes opened wide in shock.

John almost jumped out of his skin and was lost for words. He had startled this man, who must have been asleep, as much as he, himself, had been startled.

The bearded man adjusted himself and sat back where he had been before John had so rudely grabbed his feet.

John opened his mouth to speak, but stood staring ... no words came.

The bearded man pointed towards the front of the bus. 'Perhaps the trapped woman next.'

John Coyle was flustered. The bearded man was lucid and calm, appeared to have no injuries at all and was offering him advice.

'What ... Who ... ?'

'The trapped lady,' the man repeated with soft assurance.

'Why don't you get off the bus?' John finally stammered.

The man shook his head and smiled.

'My dear man. It's a very long story and I don't think you have time for a long story. Please.' Again he pointed towards the trapped woman with his arm out-stretched.

John's trance was broken by the sirens in the distance.

It was a sound that he had previously associated with apprehension. It meant trouble. Somebody was hurt, or even killed, or there was trouble for the police or a fire. But this time the sound meant something completely different. He was already in the middle of a nightmare and the sirens were the cavalry. Help was on its way. Real help. He could get off the bus, get treatment for his fingers and relax. Phone home. It was nearly over.

He had always wanted to save a life and today, he had saved many. It felt good. He started thinking about Giles Thornton and what work he might get on the 200 new homes in Southside, then he felt a sharp slap across his face.

'Young man. You've not finished yet.' The bearded man smiled again. 'The woman. She needs your help.'

John cleared his head and scanned the bus for his scaffold pole. It was half buried under rocks which had fallen towards the back of the bus when it tipped. Quickly he picked at the rocks, throwing them to the front. One of them landed on the back of the driver's seat and with a metallic sound thudded into one of the levers, which adjusted the positioning of the seat. A fraction of a second later there was a yelp as the seat sprung open like a jet pilot's ejector seat and the driver slumped to the floor.

'Jesus I love you. Thank-you, thank-you,' shouted the driver, who crawled forward and looked down at the road.

'Jump,' shouted the Greek man.

Keres did a classic double take as she looked at the front window of the bus teetering high above the edge of the road. That can't be right. Thanatos told me the driver would die. And there he is about to jump to safety.

'Jump,' shouted Ilias Vyntra.

Spiros Gekas sat on the rim of the window with his feet dangling over the edge, he eased himself forward and lowered himself a bit before rolling over and dangling with his arms and elbows resting on the rim of the window. He then lowered himself so he was dangling from his hands ... arms at full stretch.

Then he dropped and rolled in a heap on the road.

The other survivors and onlookers cheered. Spiros stood up and took a bow with a beaming smile, before walking away from his bus.

Keres was seething. If they knew the crash was his fault, they wouldn't be cheering. He's responsible for at least 16 deaths today. And he's supposed to be one of them. She quickly looked around and saw her brothers talking quietly by the row of plastic tables.

She marched over.

'Thanatos,' she blurted with venom.

He stopped mid sentence and turned to face her, alarmed by her tone.

'What's up?' He had heard the cheer, but not yet seen Spiros.

Keres pointed at him.

His face dropped. 'Oh dear.'

'Oh dear indeed. He was supposed to die. Why've you let him off?'

Thanatos stared at the driver. Keres was right. He was supposed to die. He had plans in place to take care of him whether the bus fell off the cliff or not.

'I hope you aren't goin' back on your word. You agreed the baby was safe.'

'It is Keres. It is,' He said without conviction, still staring at the driver, who was given a hero's welcome by his passengers. 'But I did plan on the driver helping me fill my quota.'

'Looks like you need a plan B.' Keres was angry.

Things were not going entirely to plan, but, although Thanatos had not wanted the driver to escape the bus, he knew things very rarely went smoothly. It was a complicated job, like many others he had done. It was important to think on your feet and react to every twist and turn with composure.

'Keres.'

She scowled at him.

'Keres. Strictly speaking, we are already on plan B, no, plan C. If you recall, I had expected Elaine White to kill off the driver. That was plan A. She chose her unborn baby instead. That was plan B. You put me under pressure and I went back to the driver. That was plan C. He's now escaped.'

'The baby lives or we are going to fall out.'

'Don't worry. We just need a plan D.'

They stood in a row, all with folded arms, watching Spiros soak up the glory after his last-gasp jump to safety.

Thanatos was deep in thought, Keres was relieved but not yet convinced that the baby would be spared, Hypnos thought it best to keep quiet while Keres was angry.

The sirens were getting close, now climbing up the cliff-top road from Palaiokastritsa, their flashing lights visible every time they turned the sharp hairpin bends of the headlands before turning away once more towards the more gentle swerves along the tree-lined slopes of the hills.

Thanatos came to a decision.

'It's gonna have to be John Coyle.'

'How ironic,' chipped in Hypnos. 'He saves the driver and has to take his place in your quota of 16 as a result.'

'Yes. Shame really. I like the bloke. I wanted him to live, but he's the only one left on the bus now, who isn't already allocated, and it's a bit late to change things.'

'Oh right,' said Keres, smiling again. 'So the bus is goin' to fall then?'

'It's gonna have to. Not much else I can do now.'

28 ... Look at their faces

25 minutes after the crash, Wednesday, April 11, 1984: 'The irritating drunk man, the

271

murderer and a fat Cockney salesman, plus one. It's not much out of 16.' Keres was hard to please.

Thanatos looked down the road, expecting emergency vehicles at any moment, then looked back at his sister.

'Come on Keres. Four's not bad. Poor Hypnos has had almost nothing to do.'

Keres looked at Hypnos with some sympathy, but still felt cheated.

Hypnos, the Greek God of Sleep and twin brother to Thanatos, the Greek God of Death, had spent most of the day serving drinks. He made no complaint, but would have liked a little more involvement.

He would have said nothing, but now was his chance. He decided against it, the sirens were too close, the job was almost over. He changed his mind and opened his mouth to speak. But didn't.

His brother noticed.

'Go on Hypnos. What?'

'Doesn't matter.'

'No. Go on.'

Hypnos looked towards the bus, then back at his brother.

'You said about a bearded man. Not hurt. Just sat back and went to sleep.'

Thanatos nodded.

'Surely that's one for me?'

Thanatos looked anxious and struggled for a good answer. The bearded man had already thrown him and he was reluctant to pass the problem on to Hypnos. That would make his control over the situation even less and that made him uncomfortable, but why shouldn't he trust his brother. It was his specialist subject.

The question was never answered as a fast response ambulance hurried around the bend and braked hard, before edging slowly past a cluster of onlookers and pulled into a passing place opposite the crashed bus. The siren was cut, but the flashing lights stayed on. It was an estate car converted for the emergency services, the back doors were thrown open and there was space for two patients on narrow bunks either side of the car.

Gordon Teal was helped into the ambulance and Geoff Miller's unconscious body was carried across the road by the driver and Ilias Vyntra. He was put on a bed and a nurse gave him pain-killers before taking a closer look at his legs.

While she focussed her attention on Geoff Miller, Gordon climbed out of the ambulance and headed slowly back towards the bus.

A second ambulance pulled up behind the first and Daisy Farrell was given treatment at the roadside.

Keres looked around confused.

'Where'd Thana go?'

Hypnos shook his head. 'Dunno.'

They both stood back and watched. The flames on the underside of the upturned bus had almost died away but it was steeply tipped over the edge of the cliff. Maybe Thanatos had gone to put the finishing touches to his work and give the bus one final push.

John Coyle was close to exhaustion. It was only adrenalin keeping him going, but he couldn't get the trapped woman out. She had passed out and her husband was firmly wedged. All John had achieved with his scaffold pole was further mutilation.

He was ready to accept defeat and save his own life but there was still the bearded man and the idiot. He threw his pole towards the front of the bus. It all helps. Come on John. One last try then get out.

He placed a hand on the bearded man's shoulder.

'Come on big man. Let's go.'

The same smile, and out-stretched arm, now pointing to the man at the back rooting through luggage.

'Try him. I'm good.'

John was losing patience and turned to the other man.

'Mate. Time's up. Gotta get off.'

No answer.

John edged a little closer, not daring to go past halfway.

'Oi! Leave it. It's not worth dying for.'

Behind John, Gordon Teal crawled back onto the bus through the smashed side window. He was alarmed to see Mary had gone. She was not where he had left her. His eyes danced around in panic until he saw her up against a twisted seat near the front of the bus. He struggled up through the debris, once again cradled her in his arms and wept.

The survivors, emergency service crew and other onlookers gasped in unison as another branch on the tree cracked loudly, the rope came free from the tree, the bus tipped to a perilous angle and slowly the van was pulled closer to the edge.

The bus had tipped almost off the cliff before very slowly tipping back again. Once more it stopped but only for a fraction of a second.

It was rocking like a seesaw, but with each swing it pulled the van closer to the edge until finally it fell over the edge with a gentle crunch, which grew louder as it gathered speed, followed closely by the van.

Before the bus crashed into the rocks at the edge of the water, the embers of the fire reached the petrol tank and there was a terrific explosion, then a brief moment of quiet before the impact at the bottom of the cliff, followed by a second impact as the van hurtled into the wreck of the bus.

The crowd was protected from the main force of the blast by the cliff, but the rush of air was still enough to knock some to the ground.

For nearly half an hour, the passengers had expected the bus to fall, but nothing could have prepared them for the enormous sense of relief they now felt as they took in the gravity of how close they had come to death.

Keres couldn't help a smile. 'I love this bit Hypno'. Look at their faces. Priceless.'

Hypnos looked around. For a few seconds the shock stunned the crowd into silence. Nobody moved. Nobody knew what to do.

The ambulance crews were first to react. One driver rushed to the edge of the cliff for a closer look. He turned to his colleagues. 'Nothing we can do for that lot. Let's get busy up here.' He raced to help his colleagues as two police cars arrived followed by a fire crew.

'Oh no Hypnos. I think we may have messed up.' Keres was looking at the cliff-top, where the bus had been. A man was lying on his side in a foetal position with a blood-soaked hand held close to his chest. A crowd started to gather. A nurse re-dressed his wounds.

Thanatos returned unruffled.

'You're in trouble.' Keres shook her head. 'Fifteen's no good. He's supposed to be dead. What happened to plan D?'

Thanatos was calm. 'Plan E.'

Keres screwed up her face in dismay. 'What?'

'Plan E is what happened to plan D.'

Keres looked scornful and waited for his explanation.

'Just before the bus fell, I saw Gordon Teal leave the ambulance. He walked over to the bus and got back on.'

Keres and Hypnos looked at each other. 'Thought you saved him.'

'I did. Looks like he over-ruled me. They were a close couple. Don't think he fancied life without Mary.'

Keres was moved. She had nothing to say. They stood in silence for a while watching the nurse treat John Coyle, before Keres asked, 'So you traded Gordon for the referee?'

Thanatos nodded, then looked towards the row of plastic tables. 'Think you have some new customers.'

The stag and his three friends played spoof at the far table with the blue umbrella.

Next to them on yellow were little Sally Whisper's parents along with the Cockney salesman, big Harry Zeng, who was joined by his wife Megan.

Then the lilac seats. Two were taken by sisters Jane and Mabel Chimera, who were still arguing. Opposite them sat the bearded man and the murderer, Pedro Raphael, who was sipping from a beer bottle while he stared at Lucy Birdham on the peach table.

Lucy sat next to Roy Farrell. They both smiled across at Mary Teal, who stood up to welcome her husband Gordon into the final place. All the seats at the tables were moulded white plastic with coloured cushions to match the umbrellas, except the final seat, which Mary stood behind beaming.

Gordon gave Mary a kiss, then made himself comfortable in his dentist chair. She passed him a bottle of beer, held his hand and pumped the seat to his preferred angle.

Behind them, at the lilac table, Keres was taking orders.

'What can I get you mister?' She didn't know the bearded man's name.

He smiled up at her, then eased his chair back and stood up. 'I'd love a beer thank-you, but give me five minutes.'

He walked down the road and round the bend.

29 ... Double Or Quits

50 minutes after the crash, Wednesday, April 11, 1984: The radio in the ambulance played Lynyrd Skynyrd Freebird.

Geoff Miller liked it. He sang along.

'If I leave here tomorrow,

'Would you still remember me?

'For I must be travelling on, now,

'Cause there's too many places I've got to see.

'But, if I stayed here with you, girl,

'Things just couldn't be the same.
'Cause I'm as free as a bird now
'And this bird you can not change.'

It was a classic. Geoff had always enjoyed the tune, but, now, for the first time, he started thinking about the words ... but only for a second before singing the next line.

He felt relaxed and comfortable. The pain-killers had kicked in and he was ready with his air guitar for the solo.

He lay on his back, drowsy, only half conscious. Looking around the ambulance in fleeting moments of clarity.

Whimpering on the other bed was the asthmatic woman ... complaining at regular intervals to the nurse and driver, both up front, every time the car hit a bump.

'Hello and welcome to Double Or Quits, live from Corfu Town on GBC1, bringing you the only show that offers life-changing prize-money of one million drachmas.

'For those of you watching for the first time,' the host laughed with forced sarcasm. 'We ask five general knowledge questions, each time doubling the prize money until we hit the sizzling sum of one million drachmas.

'Any wrong answer and you go home with nothing.

'What do you go home with?' the host shouted at his obedient audience, both arms raised with theatrical splendour.

'Nothing!' they shouted in unison.

He then swirled in dramatic flamboyance towards his first guest, before adding, 'But you can quit any time and take what you have won.'

The studio audience cheered loudly following the off-screen prompt.

The host flicked through a wad of cue cards. 'Okay. Who have we got tonight?' he asked himself out loud, before checking the cards.

'It's Geoff Miller. A painter and decorator from Southside, near London. Let's have a warm GBC1 welcome for,' and now he raised his voice, 'GEOFF MILLER.'

They went crazy for the portly foreigner.

Geoff sat dumfounded. This was a big chance. Goodbye to debt. Fresh start. He had never seen the show, but the host was familiar. Couldn't place him though.

After a few questions to settle his guest, the host slipped into his routine. 'Okay Geoff,' arm round shoulder, 'Five questions and you are a millionaire. And you can go home any time, but once I've asked the question, you MUST give me an answer.'

Geoff nodded.

'And you have two chances to phone a friend.'

Geoff nodded again.

'Who will be helping you tonight?'

Geoff stumbled on his words. He had never been on telly before. 'That would be my ex-wife Kez and ex-business partner Costa.'

'No current friends or family Geoff?' the host laughed. It was a cheap joke but the crowd loved it.

'Okay, let's hope we don't need them. Here's your first question for 62,500 drachmas.'

There was a drum roll, then silence.

'Who was the first football player to be sold for more than one million pounds?'

Geoff's eyes lit up and he blurted out the answer. 'Gerry Francis.'

'Are you sure?'

Course I'm sure fool. I'm a Forest fan and we paid the bloody money.

'Is that your final answer?'

The look of concern on the host's face started some doubt in Geoff's mind and he thought hard.

Jesus Geoff. You fucking idiot. It's Trevor Francis. Bloody think.

'No. Sorry. It's Trevor Francis.'

'Final answer?'

'Yes. Final answer.'

The host paused for dramatic effect.

'And it's the right answer. You've just won 62,500 drachmas Geoff Miller.'

There was raucous applause.

The next two questions were easy, taking Geoff up to 250,000 drachmas.

'Okay Geoff. For half a million drachmas, which is the only US state beginning with the letter P?'

Geoff screwed up his face, half closed his eyes and took a deep breath.

'I know this one. It's ...' then he was stuck. 'Can't be certain.'

'What are you thinking Geoff?' The host filled the dead air.

'Hmm ... maybe Pittsburgh,' he paused, 'or Pennsylvania ... or even Philadelphia.'

The host waited.

'I'm going to have to hurry you.'

'One of them is definitely a state, but two are cities. No. Maybe they're all cities.'

'Geoff.'

'Can I phone a friend?'

'Okay. Phone a friend. Who's it goin' to be?'

'Kez please.'

The host made the call.

'Hello. Kez Miller.'

'Hi, this is Erebos, live on GBC1 with Double Or Quits. I have Geoff Miller with me and he's stuck on 250,000 drachmas. He wants you to help him double it up to half a million.

'Okay Geoff, you have 30 seconds.'

'Hi Kez.'

'Geoff,' she groaned.

He could feel her disapproval over the phone line. He was gambling on live TV now, taking his marriage-wrecking addiction to a new level.

He reeled out the question.

'I dunno Geoff. I know the answer but it's gambling. I don't think you should be asking me.'

She went quiet.

Geoff was starting to sweat. There was a lot of money at stake. Just bloody tell me Kez. We can talk about whether it's right or wrong when the money's in the bank. He wanted to push her but knew it would have the opposite effect. He waited as the clock ticked.

'P...' she started but the line went dead.

A sharp peep sound covered Geoff's curse.

Well at least it's not Philadelphia. Kez used a hard P. Geoff was still not confident even with just two choices.

'I'll use my other phone a friend.'

The host spoke to Costa and the time started.

'Hi Costa.' Geoff gave him the question and two possible answers.

'Geoff. You've got a cheek. You've stolen thousands of pounds off me, and now you want my help?'

'Please Costa. How else can I pay you back.'

Again an awkward silence as time passed.

'Pennsylvania mate.'

'You sure?'

'Yes mate. Pennsylvania. Take care. Be good.'

The line went dead.

Geoff knew he had stolen from Costa, but he still trusted him. He was the best friend he had ever had.

'Pennsylvania. Final answer.'

'You could have gone home with 250,000 drachmas.' The host waited endlessly. 'Now you have half a million.'

The crowd went wild.

The peep machine again covered Geoff's response as he punched the air.

The applause faded as the tension grew. Geoff had a chance to answer the final question for a million drachmas.

'Half a million Geoff Miller. I think you owe Costa a beer.'

'I owe him a bit more than that,' Geoff replied with heavy irony.

'Halfway to a million drachmas.'

It was a lot of money. He needed it, but so was half a million. He could stop now. Take the money. He didn't have to do the last question. Where have I seen the host before? Anything but history. Mind you, I'm rubbish at politics too. Okay. Anything but history and politics. Too risky. No it's not. I could use a million.

'Okay Geoff Miller. You are one question away from a life-changing one million drachmas.'

The host paused.

Silence.

Another drum roll.

Silence again.

'Shall I ask question five. Do you want to try for the top prize?'

Again silence. All eyes on Geoff.

He was torn and he wanted to know why he recognised the host.

He sat with his hand rubbing his chin, staring at the host in his long orange cloak. He had a bald head and a big bushy beard. There were tattoos on the backs of his hands.

His mind raced. One million drachmas. I owe Costa a big favour. Yet again he came to my rescue when I didn't deserve it. Kez too. She didn't want to, but I'm sure she was going to give me the right answer. I'm lucky to be here at all. I should have died in the bus crash.

His line of thought stalled, stuck on the bus crash.

That's it. The show's host was on the bus.

'What's it goin' to be Geoff? Question five or take the money?'

'You were on the bus,' shouted Geoff, almost an accusation.

'Yes. I was. And now I'm with you in the ambulance.'

'No. No you're not.' Geoff thought about the ambulance. Nurse. Driver. Complaining woman. Freebird playing on the radio.

'No, you're not.' Geoff repeated.

'Take a look around.'

It was difficult lying down, but Geoff twisted his head to see the nurse in the front passenger seat looking back at the other patient. She looked anxious and was frozen, mid-sentence. The car was speeding along the road towards the city hospital but nothing moved, inside or outside. The driver was also looking back towards the other patient.

Geoff followed their gaze and saw the whining woman with her arm stretched forward and her mouth wide open stopped in the middle of what looked like a furious rant.

Then he looked beyond the driver. The road was blocked by a turning articulated lorry across their path. The ambulance driver had been distracted. They were about to collide with the lorry at high speed halfway between its front and back wheels. There was some space under the lorry, but the roof would be ripped off the ambulance.

There was a lay-by just beyond the turning lorry, empty, apart from a moulded white plastic table. It had a red umbrella and one chair ... empty with a red cushion.

Geoff thought of his mother. She often told him, when he was upset as a child, 'You look like you've found a penny and lost a pound.'

He felt like that now.

He had been here before.

The bearded man sat on the floor at the back of the ambulance between the two beds.

'It's been a long day Geoff.'

'Yes, Mr Reaper, and I thought I'd seen the last of you.'

'Sorry Geoff.'

'So. You're going back on the deal? Changed your mind?'

'No.'

'What then?'

'The deal was good. You won.'

'So why are you here?'

'Separate job. Ambulance is about to crash. Four passengers. I have a quota of one.'

'And I'm that one.'

'It could be you.'

Geoff shook his head. 'Here we go again.'

Geoff surprised himself. He should have been angry, but he found himself resigned to his fate. He had always been unlucky. Misfortune had become a habit.

He carried on shaking his head. 'So. Costa was right all along. I'm unlucky. I hoped things might even out in the long run, but no. Bad luck from start to finish.'

The Grim Reaper had no words of comfort. 'Well. I know somebody who would disagree with you. "There's no such thing as bad luck," she says, but I think you may be the exception that proves the rule. I certainly wasn't expecting to see you again. Last minute job. Infact, you are my last ever reaping job.'

'Ooh goody. That makes me feel better,' Geoff said with undisguised sarcasm, then immediately felt bad.

He lay back on his bed, before looking back at Grim.

'Last ever reaping job?'

'Yes. I've been moved on.'

'Moved on?'

'S'pose you'd call it promotion.'

Geoff nodded.

'The Grim Reaper does his job, then he'll pass them on to me.'

'Oh right.'

'There's dead people all round the island sat at white plastic tables. I'll pick them all up.'

'What? Like a bus driver taking them all to the airport.'

Grim half nodded. 'Yeah. Something like that.'

'And you'll be collecting me?'

'Well. That's up to you.'

'Go on then. What's the deal?'

'Like I said. Four people in the ambulance. I must take at least one. As things stand. You will survive.'

'But? There's always a but.'

'But the big guitar solo is about to begin in Freebird. You will be joining in with your air guitar.'

'Okay,' said Geoff, unsure where he was going.

'You've seen out the front window. We're about to crash. The lorry will take the top off the ambulance. When you thrust out your arm to play guitar, the roof will be sliced off along with your arm.'

Geoff winced and breathed in sharply.

'You will live, but...'

'So I can accept that or?'

'Accept it. Or answer the fifth question in Double Or Quits. Get the question right and you keep both arms and live. Get it wrong and you can wait at that table with the red umbrella. I'll come get you later.'

Double or quits for my left arm and I'm on my own. No more help from Costa or Kez. Anything but history or politics. I can do this.

It was a huge gamble, again, and Geoff felt the excitement growing inside him, coursing through his veins like a drug. It was irresistible ... the ultimate adrenalin buzz.

'I'm ready for the question.'

'You're taking the gamble?'

'Yes.'

'You realise that when I click my fingers, time starts again and you're going under the lorry?'

'Yes. I'm ready. Hit me Grim. Hit me with question five.'

'Okay. Good luck mate.'

Silence.

A drum roll.

Another silence.

'Who was the British Prime Minister at the outbreak of the First World War?'

'History AND politics. Fuck.'

Grim clicked his fingers.

The driver turned forward. He hit the brakes.

Something was wrong. Geoff Miller raised his head to see what was happening.

... Author's note

Garry Kay is self-published and will succeed if his readers spread the word. If you enjoyed the book, please recommend to others or buy another for a friend. A review on Amazon would be fantastic, however short. Thank-you for reading.

Printed in Great Britain
by Amazon